US Policy Towards Pakistan
1980-1988

US Policy Towards Pakistan
1980-1988

Dr Kuldip Kumar

GYAN

The Publication of this book was financially upheld by ICSSR and the responsibility of the facts stated, opinions expressed or conclusions reached are entirely that of the author and ICSSR accepts no responsibility for them.

ICSSR Consultant

Evaluated by **Professor Shashi Sahai,** Rajasthan University Jaipur.

ISBN : 978-81-212-1330-1

Price : ₹ 532

First Published, 2017

Published by

Gyan Publishing House
5, Ansari Road
Daryaganj, New Delhi-110002
Phone: 9811692060
E-mail: books@gyanbooks.com

Printed at: G. Print Process, Delhi.

Cataloging in Publication Data—DK

Courtesy: D.K. Agencies (P) Ltd. <docinfo@dkagencies.com>

Kumar, Kuldip, author.

US policy towards Pakistan, 1980-1988 / Dr Kuldip Kumar.
pages cm
Includes bibliographical references.
ISBN 9788121213301

1. United States—Foreign relations—Pakistan. 2. akistan—Foreign relations—United States. 3. United States—Foreign relations—1981-1989. I. Title.

E183.8.P18K86 2016 DDC 327.7305491 23

This Book is Dedicated to
My Mummy-Papa

Contents

Acknowledgements

The process of undertaking research that seemed necessary for writing this book has been like an expedition to the unknown. It was thrilling and exciting, but sometimes also depressing and agonizing. Nevertheless, at the end of the day, I have every reason to feel satisfied with the output of all the hard work devoted to it. At the outset, I would like to express my indebtedness to Professor Chintamani Mahapatra and Dr Mohammad Sohrab for their benign and magnanimous guidance for this book. They helped me in achieving this arduous task, so my special thanks go to them. I extend my gratitude to the library staff of Jawaharlal Nehru University (JNU), American Centre Library and IDSA Library for their valuable co-operation. My thanks are due to the loved ones who are always around me. My Special thanks to Mummy-Papa, brother Sandeep and wife Sadhna and daughter Mayra, who bear all the pain during this period and helped me in editing this book. I also thank my friends Professor Saleem Kidwai, Dr Sandeep D.K, Dr Vijay Badetiya and D.P. Lohia, they are a constant source of motivation and help in pursuing my task. Besides them, there are some others whose names are missing but they are not missing from my heart. In all, I can say that credit goes to them and mistakes are mine only.

Dr Kuldip Kumar

Introduction

The US-Pakistan relations have been quite chequered, albeit sufficiently flexible to sustain the ups and downs they have experienced so far. What have been the determining factors that have influenced their chartered course? Admittedly, relations between states are based on national interests; but it is the convergence of interests, that brings two countries close to each other and fosters co-operation. The relations between the United States and Pakistan constitute one of many contemporary instances of an alliance serving complementary interests. For the United States, it has served the main purpose of expanding the scope of the policy of containment during the Cold War; for Pakistan, it has served primarily the purpose of increasing her political, military and economic potential vis-á-vis India. This relation has of more importance for Pakistan because it sought to improve its internal economic conditions and its military capability (capabilities) against India.

The relations between these two countries have had several implications for them since the beginning. Since US was a super power and was able to help Pakistan to achieve its goals, Pakistan tried to become its faithful ally. However, US always avoided taking Pakistan's side because it gave rise to Soviet and Indian hostility. Before India's independence, the US tried to support the idea of a united India. But its relations with Pakistan have been generally cordial since the latter's formation in 1947. The initial attitude of the United States towards the creation of Pakistan was unenthusiastic. In early 1947, as events in British India were moving towards the partition of territory into India and Pakistan, the major concern of US foreign policy-makers was not South Asia. Even when the Cold War between the two superpowers was in place during this period, neither the USSR nor the US perceived major interests in the subcontinent. While Moscow regarded both India and Pakistan as Western pawns and showed little inclination towards establishing friendly ties with either country, the US had no explicit policy towards Pakistan.

As the Cold War spread, the United State's main strategy was to use Pakistan as a frontline state against the Soviet communist expansion. Various US presidents supported Pakistan by granting different kinds of economic and military assistance.Pakistan seemingly played the role of a faithful ally of the US, and sought assurance from the latter against external pressure. But the US assured help only against the communist expansion. US interest in Pakistan declined with the outbreak of the Vietnam War and Indo-Pak war, but was again restored with the Soviet communist expansion in South West Asia.After India's nuclear test explosion in 1974, Pakistan felt threatened and demanded the US help to create a Nuclear Weapon Free Zone in South Asia. The US was interested in such proposal but could do little. Pakistan continued to remain a faithful ally. Subsequently, when the US authorities came to know that Pakistan was running a secret mission to develop nuclear weapon, they did precious little to prevent it. The Carter Administration supported a tougher policy against nuclear proliferation and sought to restrict arms transfer to the developing nations. This policy of Carter was a matter of concern for Pakistan. By April 1979, the relation between two countries was an all time low because of Pakistan's secret construction of Uranium enrichment facility. When the USSR invaded Afghanistan, the US-Pakistan relations saw a major change.

Presidential aspirant Ronald Reagan was opposed to Soviet policy from the beginning. He stated in a press conference that it was important to support 'funnelling' American arms to Pakistan so that it could then trans-ship the weapon to Afghan forces as a 'signal' to the Russians that Washington was deeply concerned about the intervention. Ronald Reagan defeated Jimmy Carter in the November 1980 Presidential election, and took the oath of the office on January 20, 1981. The new administration's national security agenda included forging a closer relationship with Pakistan to make it a partner in opposing the Soviet military presence in Afghanistan. Reagan promised higher defense and other assistances to Pakistan. The US President and his top foreign policy officials stressed that Pakistan deserved far more US support than Carter had offered. They emphasised that Pakistani military forces were the largest and most experienced in Southwest Asia and Persian Gulf region, and were in short supply of modern weapons. So Washington decided to increase arms supply to Pakistan.

The US soon forged a close alliance with Pakistan to defeat Soviet Union in Afghanistan. Regan went to the extent of allowing Pakistan to carry out its nuclear programme. He agreed to allow Pakistan to continue its nuclear programme as long as it did not detonate a nuclear bomb. Pakistan achieved nuclear weapon capability in 1987. To the relief of the Pakistani leadership, Ronald Reagan's administration was willing to overlook these issues as "internal problems" of Pakistan while enlisting the latter as an ally to check Soviet advances in Afghanistan. Some prominent issues of concern in the new relationship under the presidency of Ronald Regan were Nuclear proliferation and the sale of F-16. By getting F-16 (sophisticated fighter) against all odds, Pakistan showed the world how important geo-politically it was to the US. The US supported Afghan Mujahedeens with arms and ammunition, not directly but through Pakistan channel. This only brought the two countries closer and paved the way for long-term relationship. This not only strengthened Zia-ul-Haq's position in Pakistan but also strengthened Islamic fundamentalist forces, which were eventually going to turn their guns against the US. The United States took the lead in successfully mobilising support against the Soviet invasion of Afghanistan, especially among Muslim and non-aligned countries.

The passage of Pressler Amendment was one of the significant events in the US-Pak ties during the Presidency of Reagan. In the early 1984, US intelligence reports revealed Pakistan's nuclear programme to be weapon-oriented. To express its concerns, Congress designed a new legislation to restrict the presidential waiver that Pakistan was already enjoying. The new amendment, called 'Pressler amendment', stated that no assistance, military, equipment or technology would be sold or transferred to Pakistan unless the US president certified annually that Pakistan did not posses a nuclear explosive device. The non-proliferation legislation was designed to penalise the countries involved in trafficking nuclear material from abroad. But the Pressler Amendment was country-specific, only addressing Pakistan's nuclear programme.

This book is divided into five chapters. The First chapter traces the background of US-Pakistan relations and puts them in a historical perspective. Here, important variables and basic determinants of US-Pak relations have been discussed. Second chapter seeks to focus on Ronald Reagan's policy on Afghanistan crisis; how US had used Pakistan during the Afghanistan crisis; and the benefits and losses accrued to Pakistan. The chapter also discusses the increased and decreased importance of Pakistan to the US strategy with changing circumstances in South Asia. Third chapter is concerned with the US strategy towards Pakistan during Afghan crisis. This chapter also analyses the cooperation between the two countries in military and economic areas, and also, between their intelligence agencies (CIA-ISI). It explains the role of Pakistan assigned to it by the US, to act as the frontline state against Soviet aggression. Fourth chapter is concerned with the analysis of US policy towards Pakistan that ignored nuclear proliferation. Even after knowing that Pakistan was running a secret mission to develop nuclear power, the US continued to maintain economic and military aid to Pakistan against Soviet expansion. Fifth chapter is the conclusion that examines the nature of Ronald Reagan's Policy towards Pakistan. A historical analytical method has been adopted to study this relationship.

A few primary sources and a large number of secondary sources have been consulted. This is an extremely modest exercise to understand the US policy towards Pakistan during1980-88.

Chapter 1

Historical Background of US Policy towards Pakistan (1947-1980)

Relations involving two states are largely determined by their national interests Bilateral. In fact, it is the convergence of interests that brings two countries close to each other and fosters cooperation. (http://ipripak.org/factfiles/ff28.shtml) In the light of this assumption, it can be stated that the relations between the United States and Pakistan constitute one of many contemporary instances of an alliance serving complementary interests. While for the United States, it has served primarily the purpose of expanding the scope of the policy of containment during the Cold War; for Pakistan it has served primarily the purpose of increasing her political, military and economic potential vis-á-vis India. (Morgenthau, p. 203)

When the two nation theory in British India gained popularity in the late 1930s, it had no echo in the US. The India League was active enough in lobbying in liberal circles on behalf of the Indian National Congress, but the Muslim League had no such organised group in the United States to voice its concerns about the future of the Muslim minority in post-British India. (Kux, pp. 4-5)American press focused mostly on the Indian National Congress and prominent leaders of freedom movement *viz.* Mahatma Gandhi and Jawaharlal Nehru, as the future rulers of free India. Nonetheless, some journalists were reporting about the Indian Muslim League. For example, in 1939, *The New*

York Times published a series of articles on the growing popularity of the Muslim League and Jinnah. In his widely read books titled "*Inside Asia*", John Gunther described Jinnah as one of the key leaders of the Indian sub-continent. (*ibid.* p.5). In 1940, the official American presence in India was limited to consular offices in Calcutta (Kolkata), Bombay (Mumbai), Madras (Chennai), and Karachi. There was also an American diplomatic presence in New Delhi, but official dealings with the Indian Government were handled through the British Embassy in Washington or the American Embassy in London. The US officials stationed at India undoubtedly matched political developments and sent occasional reports or "dispatches" to Washington. The Calcutta Consulate General once sent a detailed report on the Muslim League's adoption of the Pakistan resolution on April 5, 1940. A year later, another dispatch stated that the call for "Pakistan might be postponed or put aside, but it would be a mistake to dismiss the Pakistan resolution as unimportant." (*ibid*)

During World War II, Washington began to pay far more attention to India. A little before Pearl Harbour, India and the United States had opened direct diplomatic relations. In April 1942, President Franklin Roosevelt sent Louis Johnson, former assistant secretary of war, to head the Delhi mission as his "personal representative." As Japanese forces acquired Malaya and Burma and threatened to invade India, the British government offered some political concessions to the Indian nationalists to gain their cooperation in the war effort. Johnson unsuccessfully tried to broker an agreement between British envoy Sir Stafford Cripps and Congress Party leaders. It was assumed that the Muslim League, which unlike the Congress had backed the Allied war effort, would support the British proposals. (*ibid*, pp.5-6). In 1942 and 1943, a series of articles by Herbert Matthews of the *New York Times* chronicled the wartime rise in the Muslim League's popularity and the pivotal role that its leader would play in deciding India's future. On October 4, 1942, an article headlined "Jinnah Holds the Key to Peace in India" observed, "Out of the throes of Indian travail a new figure has arisen and he holds in his hands more power for good or evil than any single Indian politician. It is that tall, thin, exasperatingly deliberate man who seems to be taking pleasure at keeping the world guessing,Mohammed Ali Jinnah. In his delicate hands lies the answer to the riddle: Can Hindus and Moslems agree?" (*ibid*). President Roosevelt was not in favour of the idea of dividing India. The partition of India "sounded terrible" to American ears after the experience of the US civil war. However, US diplomat William Phillips, who had replaced Johnson as Roosevelt's personal representative, spent nearly four hours with Jinnah in early 1943 at the latter's home in New Delhi and found Jinnah "brilliant". While he was "attracted to him personally," he was opposed to partition. Phillips later wrote in his memoirs, "The more I studied Mr Jinnah's Pakistan, the less it appealed to me as the answer to India's communal problem, since to break India into two separate nations would weaken both and might open Pakistan, at least, to the designs of ambitious neighbours." (*ibid*, pp. 6-7)

As the war progressed, India became a major supply base of allied powers for sending military equipment to China and for preparing for the recon quest of Burma. Some 350,000 American troops were stationed in India, principally as quartermasters and engineers functioning in Bengal and Assam. Worried that nationalists might interpret the large US military presence as a sign of political support for the British, an official statement by the Roosevelt Administration issued on August 12, 1942, stressed that the American forces were in India only to fight the war against the Axis Powers. (*ibid,* p. 7). Even though US diplomats avoided taking sides, they followed political developments in India closely and kept in touch with the major political groups, including the Muslim League. One of the most frequent callers on Jinnah was John Davies, Jr, a China specialist and a former political adviser to General Joseph.

W Stilwell, the US commander of the China-Burma-India Theater. Davies was impersonal with Jinnah's acumen, but thought that Jinnah doubted that he would actually attain his goal of Pakistan, which was initially devised for bargaining purposes to gain political leverage for the Muslims. In January 1945, the US State Department publicly called for a political settlement among the British, the Congress and the League; and offered to help the process along. When Secretary of State Edward Stettinius met British foreign secretary Anthony Eden in April 1945, he urged Britain to move India toward self-rule. Stettinius told Eden that Allied "prestige in the Far East be greatly improved whenever a solution to the problem of India is found". Eden responded by expressing doubt whether the Indian problem would be solved as long as Gandhi remained alive. (*ibid*, p. 7)

In 1946, the American mission in New Delhi supported British efforts to maintain a united India. A US diplomat, for example, warned Liaquat Ali Khan, Jinnah's chief lieutenant, that a continued hard-line attitude by the League on the Cabinet Mission Plan would cost it America's sympathy. Although the impact of the warning is not clear, the Muslim League agreed to the British proposal for a united India with weak central and strong regional governments. It appreciated that Jinnah played his cards skilfully. The US mission in India reported to Washington that Jinnah's greatest triumph was reflected in blocking India's road to independence. The adamant attitude of Jinnah and the Muslim League to create a separate country for Muslims led to massive violence in most parts of India. Disturbed by the rapidly deteriorating situation, the State Department backed the British efforts to reach a political settlement. On August 27, 1946, Acting Secretary of State Dean Acheson declared that the United States offered its "best wishes" to the Indian interim government, expressed regret "that the Muslim League has not decided to participate," and hoped "that it may later find it possible to do so" (*ibid*, pp. 9-10). To bolster the interim government's prestige, Washington established full diplomatic relations with India, transforming the US mission in New Delhi into an embassy before the British granted formal independence. Henry Grady, a former Assistant Secretary of State and the leader of a 1942 wartime economic mission to India, was named the first US ambassador to India.

While establishing diplomatic ties with India, the Truman Administration did not maintain distance from the Muslim League. On November 14, 1946, the first official contact in Washington with the Muslim League took place. After failing to meet President Truman, MAH Ispahani, a Calcutta businessman close to Jinnah, and later Pakistan's first ambassador to the United States, and Begum Shah Nawaz, a prominent Punjabi personality, met Dean Acheson and explained the case of Pakistan. The US diplomat avoided taking a substantive stance. Ispahani and Begum Shah Nawaz then participated in a New York Herald Tribune forum on the future of India and travelled throughout the United States to "promote Pakistan" among prominent Americans. (*ibid*)

Although the Muslim League eventually joined the interim government, the political deadlock and communal violence continued. Fear of possible civil war in India and "perhaps at the same time a revolutionary war against the remnants of British power" spurred State Department officials to recommend in late November 1946, American pressure for an early agreement between the Muslim League and the Congress. As 1946 drew to a close, British Prime Minister Clement Attlee summoned Nehru and Jinnah to London in a desperate attempt to break the impasse. In support of the effort, the State Department instructed the London embassy to "impress on Indian leaders...deep interest" of the United States in the "successful conclusion of talks." (*ibid*, pp. 10-11). Although the London talks failed, the State Department continued to press for an agreement between the Congress and the League, instructing the New Delhi embassy to urge the Muslim League to cooperate with the Congress within the framework proposed by the British. (*ibid*, p. 11)

Since 1947, "containment deliberately designed to check the expansion of communism" became the principal objective of the US foreign policy, as a result of which "for a decade and a half after the Second World War, the United States identified its security with alliance." And as the Cold War spread to Asia, the United States badly felt the need of an ally so as to bridge the gap in its security system vis-á-vis the communist world. (Chopra, Surendra, p. 32). During this troubled period, US diplomat Raymond Hare, who was scheduled to head the State Department's South Asia division, spent two months in the subcontinent to have a firsthand understanding of his new area of responsibility. During his travels, he spoke with all the top leaders, including Jinnah, whom he met for an hour and a half in New Delhi on May 1, 1947. Jinnah asserted that creation of Pakistan would clear the communal atmosphere and reduce tensions, a position that Hare did not share. Responding to Hare's query about the country's foreign policy, Jinnah said that Pakistan would be oriented toward the Muslim countries of the Middle East, which "would stand together against possible Russian aggression and would look to the US for assistance". (Kux, pp. 12-13). Ultimately, when the British Government decided to partition India and establish a new state of Pakistan, the US did differ to prevent this. When the Cold War tension spread and the US looked for allies, India turned out to be a champion of the non-alignment, while Pakistan was willing to be an alliance partner.However, the United States and Pakistan had divergent goals and interests in forging in an alliance. For Pakistan, the main consideration in forging a security relationship with US was its obsession with the perceived threat from India; and its desire to procure by means of an alliance substantial economic aid to accelerate economic development and military assistance so as to improve its defence capabilities vis-á-vis India. (Jain, Rashmi, 1983, p.18)

The United States simply had no major interests in the subcontinent. In part, this was explained by the fact that the region stood apart from the Cold War struggle with the Soviet Union, which was already dominating US foreign policy. Moscow regarded both India and Pakistan as Western pawns and showed little inclination to establish friendly ties with either country (*ibid*, pp.16-17). In the immediate aftermath of the emergence of India and Pakistan as sovereign nations, American policy-makers approached South Asia primarily governed by British advice. American interest in sub-continental affairs was marginal. European economic recovery, the military resurgence of Western Europe, and the containment of Soviet "expansionism" were accorded the greatest priority. Between India and Pakistan, however, Washington attached greater importance to the former apparently because it was larger in size and population, and had considerable economic and military potential. The relatively low level of American interest in Pakistan during 1947-49 was evident from tardiness in appointing an Ambassador to Pakistan. (Jain, Rashmi, 1983, p. 1-2)

As the Cold War unfolded, Pakistan leaned toward the West. Jinnah plainly spelt out that communism would not flourish on the soil of Islam. And that Pakistan's interests were more in common with the "two great democratic countries, namely, the UK and the USA, rather than with Russia". From the start, therefore, Pakistan's orientation differed from that of India, which professed non-alignment. Practical considerations bolstered Pakistan's pro-western orientation. The financially strapped country badly needed help and was not bashful about seeking it from the United States. Barely two weeks after Pakistan's independence, Finance Minister Ghulam Mohammed sounded out US Charge d'Affaires Charles Lewis regarding possible aid. In September 1947, during cabinet meeting, Jinnah outlined Pakistan's case-in effect, a Cold War version of the "Great Game" between imperial Russia and British India. "The safety of the North West Frontier was the world's concern and not merely an internal matter for Pakistan alone," Jinnah stated (*ibid*, pp. 20-21). He believed that the Russians were behind the Afghan call for Pushtonistan. "In this connection," Jinnah added, "it is significant to note that Russia alone of all the great countries has not sent a congratulatory message on the birth of Pakistan" (*ibid*). Washington's attention was fixed on Europe, the Middle East, and China; South Asia remained on the periphery of the US worldview. On December 17, 1947, Acting Secretary of State Robert J Smith responded with a polite, but near total turn down. In the end, Pakistan received a $10 million relief grant from the War Assets Administration, or 0.5 per cent of its request (*ibid*).

With Harry S Truman in the White House, the United States sought good relations with both Pakistan and India, and tried to avoid taking sides with either of the two countries. The principal American goal in the sub-continent was to solve the Kashmir dispute in order to prevent further instability in South Asia. The memory of the communal horrors of 1946 and 1947 remained vividly in the collective mind. Since the Soviet Union kept largely aloof from the region, Cold War considerations were not the major factors in the US policy, except with regard to Pakistan's troubles with Afghanistan. (*ibid*, p. 49) In January 1953, Dwight Eisenhower became the first Republican President of the United States in twenty years. During the election, he had promised a tougher national security policy with greater reliance on collective security pacts to contain the Soviet bloc. Although South Asia was not the focus of special attention during the campaign, Republican rhetoric stirred hopes in Pakistan that the quest for US military aid might at last bear fruit. Eisenhower's selection of John Foster Dulles as secretary of state was also good news for Pakistan. The new secretary combined a passion for foreign affairs and strong streak of Calvinist morality that reflected his family background (*ibid*, p. 51). Dulles had no firsthand knowledge of South Asia, however, and prior to 1953, had apparently read only two books about the subcontinent. One was "*Life in India*", a mid-Victorian eulogy to the virtues of British colonial rule. The author was Rev John Welsh Dulles, the new secretary's grandfather. The other book was Jawaharlal Nehru's "*Glimpses of World History*", which the future Indian prime minister had written to his daughter, Indira, from jail during the 1930s. Nehru's agnostic and socialist views hardly impressed the profoundly religious and deeply anti-communist Dulles. By the time he became secretary of state, Dulles had already formed an unfavourable impression of India and a favourable one of Pakistan. He found Nehru's "neutralist foreign policy" naive, if not unprincipled, and liked Pakistan's anti-communist orientation. It was Pakistan's economic weakness that was on display when Zafrullah Khan (Pakistan's Foreign Minister) strode into the State Department on January 23, 1953, to request emergency wheat shipments in order to avert a grave food shortage. (*ibid.*, pp. 51-52)

When Eisenhower became president in 1953, US policy emphasised strengthening the collective security cordon around the communist bloc. In the case of South Asia, this meant enlisting an only too willing Pakistan as a partner in bolstering the defence of the Middle East. Even though Washington realised that the move would strain relations with larger India, the step was deemed worthwhile. But the United States and Pakistan entered into the alliance for different and essentially conflicting reasons. Despite its anti-communist orientation, Pakistan remained concerned at heart about the threat from India rather than any menace from the communists. In contrast, the United States saw the security accord as directed strictly against the communist threat and was wary of becoming entangled in Pakistan's dispute with India. (*ibid.*, pp. 84-85). The announcement of military aid to Pakistan was made on February 25, 1954, i.e. soon after Pakistan demonstrated its "resolve to play an important part in the collective defence of the free world", by signing a friendship treaty with Turkey. The announcement of military aid was followed in quick succession by signing of the US-Pakistan Mutual Defence Agreement on May 19, 1954 and the formation of the South East Asia Treaty Organisation (SEATO) in September 1954 and the Baghdad Pact in 1955.

Pakistan had aspired for the creation of a strong regional grouping in Asia on the NATO pattern. The United States, however, hesitated to commit the necessary forces and was opposed to the appointment of an Allied Commander to the Middle East or Southeast Asia. American military commitments to Pakistan were qualified in two significant respects. Unlike its military obligation to member states of NATO, the United States did not bind itself to consider automatically any attack on Pakistan as an attack on itself, and only agreed to meet the common danger in accordance with respective constitutional processes. Washington was clear that its commitments would "apply only to communist aggression". Moreover, unlike

SEATO, the United States did not officially sign the Baghdad Pact primarily because it did not wish its adherence to cause further estrangement with Egypt and its Arab allies; and did not want Israel to put forward a counter demand for a mutual defence treaty on grounds of America's alliance with Iraq, a member of the Arab League. (Rashmi Jain, pp. 11-12)

By January 1957, the end of Eisenhower's first term, these fundamentally divergent aims were apparent in both Karachi and Washington, even if US and Pakistani leaders preferred to sweep their differences under the rug. Although Washington was aware that the original rationale for military aid for Pakistan was flawed and that even with US help Pakistan was unlikely to contribute to Middle East defence, little could be undone. The US government however, remained warm in its public praise of Pakistan as a faithful ally. Pakistan on its part remained committed to the course it had chosen as the best means of improving Pakistan's security against India. In his second inaugural address on January 24, 1957, President Eisenhower expressed his concern that communism would prove attractive to newly independent nations unless they achieved more rapid economic development. "New forces and new nations are stirring across the earth," the President declared. To counter the Soviets more effectively, Eisenhower asked for a substantial increase in foreign assistance, arguing that this was in the US national interest. In practice, these views of the president translated into a new focus for US policy toward South Asia, one that placed greater emphasis during Eisenhower's second term on bolstering India's economic development than on strengthening Pakistan's defence forces. The change was gradual, but still unsettling to Pakistan, which began to complain that the United States was favouring non-aligned India over Pakistan. Unhappiness over alignment with the west, already strong in intellectual circles, gained ground in Pakistan; while rival India basked in international prominence as the leader of the emerging non-aligned bloc, courted by both the United States and the Soviet Union. In contrast, a number of Middle Eastern Muslim countries criticised Pakistan as a US camp follower that had bartered its foreign policy independence for a pot of American arms. (Kux., pp. 84-86)

In 1959, Dwight Eisenhower became the first US President to visit Pakistan. Earlier, in the fall of 1959, Ayub Khan had announced measures designed to move his country slowly towards his version of democracy. He established a system of local councils, called "basic democracies," elected by universal suffrage. About eighty thousand "basic democrats" became a national electoral college that would select a national assembly in 1962 and elect a president in 1965. (Kux, pp.106-7) When Dwight Eisenhower left the White House in January 1961, he was happy that the US's ally Pakistan appeared to be getting on its feet under Ayub Khan and was beginning to make tangible economic progress. Pakistan also was moving slowly from a military dictatorship towards the establishment of a relatively more open political system. Although Pakistani people in remained extremely unhappy about growing US support for India's economic development, the US-Pakistan bilateral relations were growing too. The US continued to provide substantial economic and arms aid to Pakistan, including the promised provision of the controversial F-104 fighters. Despite the U-2 episode, Pakistan appeared to be a reliable member of the anti-communist team. US-India relations had also become increasingly friendly during Eisenhower's second term, as they improved from the low point reached following the decision to enter into an alliance with Pakistan. On the surface, the Eisenhower administration had achieved the long-standing American goal of having good relations with both India and Pakistan. But in spite of appearances, the quick sands on which the security ties with Pakistan stood would become apparent during the presidency of Eisenhower's successor. The response of John F Kennedy to the 1962 Sino-Indian border conflict would unhinge the US-Pakistan partnership. (Kux, p.114)

Pakistan closely followed the 1960 US presidential elections. It considered former Vice-President Richard Nixon, the Republican candidate, a friend and was worried that John F Kennedy, his Democratic challenger, would accelerate the policy shift towards India. The senator from Massachusetts had sharply criticised John Foster Dulles's penchant for military pacts with the Third World states. In an influential October 1957 *Foreign Affairs* article, Kennedy supported more cooperative relations with the nations of the "uncommitted world" and supported for a major boost in economic assistance to India. A resolution endorsing increased aid for India, jointly sponsored by Kennedy and Senator John Sherman Cooper (R-Ky), a former ambassador to New Delhi, was adopted by the Senate in 1958 and by both houses of Congress in 1959. After Kennedy became President, Pakistan had more tangible grounds for concern. In his State of the Union address to Congress on January 30, 1961, Kennedy lauded the "soaring idealism" of Jawaharlal Nehru, whom he praised as one of the great leaders of the twentieth century. The new administration's foreign policy and diplomatic appointees were unusually knowledgeable about South Asia, and Pakistan feared increased US tilt towards India. (Kux, p.115)

Kennedy himself remained interested and involved in South Asia throughout his presidency. Whereas Eisenhower, who also had paid considerable attention to the subcontinent, usually dealt at the level of high policy, Kennedy liked to plunge into the details. Reflecting his personal style, the new president frequently bypassed the normal bureaucratic chain of command to telephone State Department specialists and discuss current issues. Kennedy held numerous operational sessions on the region with senior advisers from the NSC, the Departments of State and Defence, and the CIA. The door to the Oval Office was open to visitors from India and Pakistan, as well as to their ambassadors in Washington. Worried about a further shift in US policy, Pakistan President Ayub Khan sent his finance minister, Mohammed Shoaib, to Washington within weeks of Kennedy's taking office. On March 7, 1961, Shoaib presented the new president a short but pointed message from Ayub reaffirming that Pakistan's "destiny lies in friendship with the United States." Kennedy responded positively. Two weeks later, Averell Harriman, whom Kennedy had appointed as a roving ambassador, met Ayub in Karachi to estabilsh closer contact.

(Kux, p.116). Although Ayub added that he did not oppose Kennedy's desire for better relations with non-aligned countries, such as India, he urged Washington to "maintain distinction between the non-aligned countries and Pakistan." Ayub stressed that the "focal point of Pakistan's policy was the continued friendship with" the United States. He also indicated that he was trying to establish more normal relations with China and also with the Soviet Union. Ever since the U-2 incident, Ayub had been trying to increase Pakistan's manoeuvring space in the field of foreign policy and reduce its near total dependence on the United States. (Kux, p.117). In July 1961, Ayub paid his first official visit to the United States as President of Pakistan. Defining Pakistan's feelings towards the United States as "not so much anger as disappointment", Ayub openly tried with the idea of re-examining membership in the Southeast Asia Treaty Organisation (SEATO) in an interview with Associated Press correspondent Jim Becker. (Kux, p.120)

During the state visit, he also discussed his country's troubled relations with Afghanistan. He told Kennedy that Kabul regime had mortgaged its future to the Soviets and urged the United States to adopt a tough line. Kennedy did not agree with Ayub's position on the ground that this approach would only push the Afghans closer to the Soviet camp. (Kux, pp. 124-125). The following year at a press conference, President Kennedy succinctly summed up the US policy dilemma in South Asia "I can tell you that there's nothing that has occupied our attention more over the last nine months." Although the United States wanted to help India against the Chinese, "everything we give to India adversely affects the balance of power with Pakistan so we are dealing with a very complicated problem because the hostility between them is so deep." (Kux, p.146) The United States had hoped for a Kashmir settlement, Kennedy continued, "but Kashmir is farther from being settled today than it was six months ago. So we were trying to balance off what is one of our more difficult problems." In October 1963, Foreign Minister Bhutto, whom Washington by then considered an unhelpful hawk on India, pro-Chinese, and anti-American, visited the White House. After his talk with

Kennedy, Bhutto accepted the US President's suggestion that General Maxwell Taylor, chairman of the Joint Chiefs of Staff would visit Pakistan to examine "the measures which we could take that might tend to reassure Pakistan about our support in the event of an attack on it by India." By the time General Taylor travelled to Pakistan in December 1963, Kennedy was dead, and Lyndon B Johnson had become President of the United States. At the time of Kennedy's assassination, the US-Pakistan alliance was beginning to unravel. Kennedy was bent on providing long-term military aid to India and seemed willing to accept the consequences in terms of further trouble with Pakistan. In turn, Ayub did not want to lose US assistance, but seemed set on moving towards friendlier relations with China, an action Washington regarded as contrary to US interests and Pakistan's alliance obligations. Kennedy, however, was willing to accept Ayub's contention that US military aid to India hurt Pakistan's security interests. (*ibid*)

The Johnson years witnessed a fundamental shift in US-Pakistan relations. When Johnson became president after Kennedy's assassination, the bilateral relations were at a "standoff" over US military aid to India and Pakistan's flirtation with China. President Johnson sought to limit Pakistan's relations with China as the price for continued large-scale US economic aid. When the pressure tactics failed and Pakistan and India went to war over Kashmir in 1965, Johnson largely gave up on Pakistan. This was reflected in US position of neutrality in India-Pak war. Washington responded by taking the side of Pakistan and rather imposed arms embargo against its alliance partner. With the Vietnam War at its peak, the United States lost interest in the subcontinent. By the time Johnson left office in January 1969, the alliance was over in all but name and the United States was no longer trying to serve as South Asia's security manager. Even though Washington continued to provide substantial economic assistance, it had drastically restricted the military supply. (Kux, p.176)

As the alliance relationship nose-dived, the one substantial facility that Pakistan had provided the Americans, the Badaber intelligence facility, was closed down. For all practical purposes, the US-Pakistan alliance had become a notional affair by the time Pakistan's old friend Richard Nixon defeated Vice-President Hubert Humphrey in the 1968 Presidential elections. In January 1969, when Nixon became President, Ayub's regime was crumbling. To maintain order in the streets against anti-government demonstrators, the Pakistan President found it necessary to deploy the army in Karachi, Lahore, Dacca, and other major cities. Ayub's willingness to negotiate with opposition leaders, not to run in the 1970 elections, and to shift from a presidential to a parliamentary system failed to restore calm. (Kux, pp. 177-178)

US-Pakistan relations had dramatically deteriorated during two previous administrations. But when Richard Nixon moved into the White House, Islamabad had reason to hope for better days. An old friend of Pakistan, Nixon had visited the country five times, twice as Vice-president and three times after he left that office. Ayub had wisely given Nixon a red carpet during his travels as a private citizen. In contrast, the Indians received him with the minimum courtesy consistent with protocol. Nixon was "grateful for the courtesies" extended to him during his visits to Pakistan. But as Nixon settled into the presidency, he continued the South Asia policy that he inherited, "except to adopt a somewhat warmer tone towards Pakistan." In Asia, the Nixon administration's major goal was to disengage US military forces from Vietnam without appearing to lose the war. (Kux, p.179)

It was during the Nixon years In the White House that Ayub Khan tumbled from power. His successor, Yahya Khan, lacked the acumen to manage his country's delicate political situation and blundered in using force to try to crush East Pakistani aspirations. During 1971, the coincidence of the East Pakistan crisis and Nixon's China initiative placed South Asia at the centre of US foreign policy concerns. Tilting towards Pakistan, Nixon sought to protect the opening to China and to prevent what he feared would be a major Soviet gain in the balance of power in Asia. A fundamental misread of the India-Pakistan situation, Nixon's tilt had little effect on the crisis but resulted in an embarrassing US diplomatic setback. President Nixon could do little of a new nation called Bangladesh. (Kux, p. 213)

In 1973, Richard Nixon appointed Gerald Ford, the Republican leader in the House of Representatives, as Vice-president after Spiro Agnew resigned rather than face prosecution on charges of corruption. A year later, when Nixon himself resigned, Ford became the next President of the US. (Kux, p. 215). The two and a half years of Gerald Ford's presidency saw a continuation of Nixon's policy of warm relations with Pakistan. Even though Islamabad had left SEATO in 1972 and remained only a nominal member of CENTO, the Ford administration considered Pakistan a good friend and ally. Still, lingering congressional antipathy because of Pakistan's conduct in 1971 delayed lifting the decade-old embargo on lethal arms transfers until February 1975. Moreover, when President Ford removed the restrictions, he failed to restore the intimate pre-1965 US-Pakistan security relationship. (Kux, p. 225)

The United States had few disputes with Bhutto's efforts to strengthen Pakistan's ties with Muslim countries and to play a larger role in the Third World. In the case of China, Pakistan's close ties paralleled Washington's was own entente with Beijing. The only significant bilateral problem was related to the nuclear issue due to Pakistan's efforts to match India's nuclear explosive capability, particularly since India's first nuclear test in 1974. Deterring Pakistan from pursuing the nuclear path soon become a major end, at times, the dominant bilateral issue during the remaining decades of the twentieth century. Pakistan's nuclear policy made clear that it was willing to risk serious problems with the United States in the effort to acquire its own deterrent. (Kux, p. 226)

In 1974, the Agency for International Development proposed a loan of $7.6 million and about $300,000 yearly in dollar grants over the next five years for the development of a national agricultural research network; loan of about $30 million in 1975 for the construction of a plant to manufacture urea from Pakistan's abundant supplies of natural gas, and another $ 15 million aid loan to modernise cotton seed oil extraction plants. But, while the United States appeared sympathetic to Pakistan's economic needs, till as late as the middle of 1974, it was not inclined to make changes in its arms policy towards the subcontinent or allay Pakistan's apprehensions about India's intentions which were intensified after the Indian Pokharan explosion. India's peaceful nuclear explosion of an atomic device in May 1974 was considered by ZA Bhutto as upsetting the balance and peace in the subcontinent and as posing as a grave threat to Pakistan's security. In the wake of India's peaceful nuclear explosion, Bhutto adopted a multi-pronged approach. Firstly, he sought some sort of a guarantee or assurance against the nuclear threat posed by India from all five nuclear weapon states of failing that at least form one of them (employing the US). The United States, however, was disinterested in providing any such guarantee. Secondly, Islamabad sought international support for the creation of a Nuclear Weapon Free Zone (NWFZ) in South Asia. Thirdly, Pakistan exerted pressure on the United States to lift the arms embargo and to provide sophisticated military equipment for strengthening its conventional armed forces as India's nuclear explosion was considered as constituting more of apolitical than a military instrument of intimidation and India was seen as posing more of a conventional, rather than a nuclear and military threat in the near future. Lastly, Pakistan, at the same time, intensified its nuclear progamme (Rashmi Jain, 1983, pp. 45-46). While the United States believed that the establishment of NWFZ, which satisfied the fourfold criteria, could make a substantial contribution to non-proliferation and to regional stability and security, it found difficult to take the side of Pakistan against India, and adopted a non-partisan attitude on the issue, abstaining on both resolutions which were adopted by the UN General Assembly.

During 1975 and again in 1976, the United States abstained on Pakistan's resolution on NWFZ in South Asia (Rashmi Jain, 1983, p. 47). Pakistan had a reason to be uneasy about Jimmy Carter's arrival in the White House. Ford's defeat meant the departure of Secretary of State, Henry Kissinger, with whom Islamabad had developed a close working relationship. Islamabad worried that the policies that Carter had advocated during the election reflected a tougher nuclear non-proliferation stance, a more restrictive approach to arms transfers to nations of the developing world, and a greater emphasis on human rights would not augur well for US-Pakistan relations. (Kux, p. 227) The assumption of Presidency by Jimmy Carter in 1977 created apprehensions in Pakistan about the future of US-Pak relations because of the Democrat's known unfavourable views on arms sales and nuclear proliferation. In fact, in contrast to the US "tilt" towards Pakistan in the early 1970s the downward trend in the relations between the two countries, which started after the lifting of the arms embargo in February 1975, became even more evident during the Carter Administration and reached an all-time low in April 1979. It was only in the wake of the Soviet intervention in Afghanistan in December 1979 that the United States "rediscovered" the strategic importance of Pakistan and sought to extend economic and military assistance to Pakistan in order to safeguard its interests in South-West Asia, especially in the Persian Gulf. When Carter assumed office in 1977, Pakistan rarely blipped on US policy agenda. The US importance it had enjoyed as a link in Dulles chain of containment had long since faded (Rashmi Jain, 1983, p. 65). Pakistan's other key asset in its relations with the United States in the Nixon years had disappeared since Washington now had direct access to China (*ibid,* p. 66).

The US aid to Pakistan was suspended by the Carter Administration in April 1979, under Section 669 of the Foreign Assistance Act (FAA), because of Pakistan's secret construction of a uranium enrichment facility. (http://www.fas.org) A number of United States laws, amendments to the Foreign Assistance Act of 1961, applied to Pakistan and its programme of nuclear weapons development. The 1976 Symington Amendment stipulated that economic assistance be terminated to any country that imported uranium enrichment technology. The Glenn Amendment of 1977 similarly called for an end to aid to countries that imported reprocessing technology,Pakistan had from France. United States economic assistance, except for food aid, was terminated under the Symington Amendment in April 1979. (http://www.country-data.com/cgi-bin/query/r-9889.html), Following the Soviet invasion of Afghanistan in December 1979, Pakistan came to be viewed as a frontline state against Soviet expansionism. (http://www.fas.org) "Earlier, Pakistan had little involvement in Afghanistan, accepting, as did the US, that it was on the margins of the Soviet sphere of influence. But following the Soviet invasion of Afghanistan, Pakistan's then military regime eagerly accepted Washington's demand that Pakistan serve as the frontline state in what proved to be the last great Cold War confrontation (*ibid*). An offer to Pakistan of $400 million in economic and security aid by the Carter Administration in early 1980 was turned down by President Zia-ul-Haq as 'peanuts'. In September 1981, however, the Reagan Administration, negotiated a $3.2 billion, five-year economic and military aid package with Pakistan. Congress facilitated the resumption of aid in December by adding Section 620E to the FAA, giving the President authority to waive Section 669 for six years in the case of Pakistan, on grounds of national interest. Pakistan became a funnel for arms supplies to the Afghan resistance, as well as a camp for three million Afghan refugees. (*ibid*) "US support enabled Zia-ul-Huq, who in 1977 had overthrown a populist regime that initially derived much of its support from Pakistan's impoverished masses, to consolidate his right-wing dictatorship and re-equip Pakistan's military. The US also encouraged the oil sheikdoms of the Persian Gulf to funnel large sums to Pakistan, its religious organisations and the Afghan opposition. The Pakistani intelligence service, the Inter Services Intelligence Agency (ISI), became increasingly important as it served as the nexus for funding the US-backed, Islamic fundamentalist Afghan opposition. Through their Afghan connections, ISI leaders soon developed a major financial interest in the country's drug and small-arms trade. (http://www.wsws.org/). "The resentment of many Pakistanis for the US support of Zia-ul-Huq and for Pakistan's US-directed intervention in the Afghan civil war is typified by the following comment from a Pakistani journalist:

What handsome revenge for America's debacle in Vietnam was the savaging of the Soviet bear in Afghanistan. A handful of Pakistani generals enriched themselves during that momentous struggle. But what did the country get? Guns, violence, drugs and a sea of refugees. All the glory America's, all the recurring costs Pakistan's. Anyone could be forgiven for thinking that history was being repeated. (http://www.wsws.org/). The Pakistan-US relationship in the fifth decade of its existence, has evolved over the successive phases of Cold War and detente and, since its inception, has been characterised by numerous "ups tilt" disenchantment, and then realignment have been the hallmarks of this bilateral relationship.(Iftikhar H. Mallik (1990), *Asian Survey*, Vol. xxx, No. 3 March 1990, p. 284)

The Soviet Union, meanwhile, under its new leader, Mikhail S Gorbachev, was reassessing its role in Afghanistan. Indirect "proximity" negotiations in Geneva under the auspices of the UN were going on between Afghanistan and Pakistan with the United States and the Soviet Union as observers. In April 1988, a series of agreements were signed among the United States, the Soviet Union, Pakistan, and Afghanistan that called for the withdrawal of Soviet forces by mid-February 1989. The withdrawal was completed on time. Throughout the years of Soviet occupation of Afghanistan, relations between the United States and Pakistan were best characterised by close cooperation. Still, United States policy makers became increasingly concerned that Zia and his associates-most notably, General Akhtar Abdur Rahman, then head of the Directorate for Inter-Services Intelligence,appeared to give preferential treatment to the Islamic fundamentalists, especially Mujahidin leader Gulbuddin Hikmatyar. Other disagreements persisted, particularly over the failure of the Zia regime to convert to representative government. Documented violations of human rights in Pakistan were another major issue; Pakistani involvement in narcotics trafficking was yet another. But the issue that after Zia's death led to another cut off of aid was Pakistan's persistent drive towards nuclear development. (http://www.country-data.com/cgi-bin/query/r- 9889.html)

References

http://ipripak.org/factfiles/ff28.shtml

Morgenthaw, Hans J. and by Kenneth W. Thompson, Political Among Nations: The Struggle for the Power and Peace, Kalyani Publishers, New Delhi- Ludhiyana.

Kissinger, Henry (1979), *White House Years*, Boston: Little Brown.

Ahmad, Mushtaq (1968), *Pakistan's Foreign Policy*, Karachi.

Ahmad, Mushtaq (1968), *Pakistan's Foreign Policy*, Karachi.

Amnesty International Report (1986), London: Amnesty International Publications, 1986.

Arms for Rebels Siphoned Off, Washington Post, January 16, 1986.

Brands, W.J. (1972), India, Pakistan and the Great Powers, New York.

Brzezinski, Zbigniew (1986), Power and Principle: Memoirs of the National Security Adviser:1977-1981, New York: Farrar, Straus, Giroux.

Chatterjee, Partha (1999), "Fragile Distinctions: Between Good and Bad Nationalism", *The Times of India*, New Delhi, 20 August 1999.

Chopra, Surendra (1983), *Perspectives on Pakistan's Foreign Policy*, Amritsar: Guru Nanak Dev University Press.

Christopher Layne, "The Real Conservative Agenda," Foreign Policy (Winter 1985-1986), pp. 73-93.

H. Mallik, Iftikhar, (1990) *"The Pakistan-US Security relationship", Asian Survey*, Vol. xxx, No. 3, March 1990.

Harrison, Selig (1986), "Cut a Regional Deal," *Foreign Policy* (spring), 1986.

http://cns.miis.edu/research/wtc01/pak.htm

http://cns.miis.edu/research/wtc01/pak.htm

http://www.country-data.com/cgi-bin/query/r-9889.html

http://www.country-data.com/cgi-bin/query/r-9889.html

http://www.country-data.com/cgi-bin/query/r-9896.htm

http://www.country-data.com/cgi-bin/query/r-9896.htm

http://www.fas.org

http://www.fas.org/

http://www.wsws.org

http://www.wsws.org/

Jain, Rajendra K.(eds) (1983), *US-South Asian Relations: 1947-82*, Vol. 2, New Delhi, Radiant Publication.

Jain, Rashmi (1983), *US-Pak Relations 1947-1983*, New Delhi: Radiant.

James N. Rasenau and others, World Politics, New York, 1976, p. 35.

Karp, Craig M. (1986), "The War in Afghanistan," *Foreign Affairs*, (summer), 1986.

Kux,Dennis (2001), *The United States and Pakistan: 1947-2000*, Washington D.C.: Woodrow Wilson Centre Press.

Layne, Christopher (1985-86), "The Real Conservative Agenda," *Foreign Policy* Winter, 1985-1986).

Mallik, Iftikhar H. (1990), *Asian Survey*, Vol. xxx, No. 3 March 1990.

N. Rasenau, James and others (1976), *World Politics*, New York.

Pincus, Walter (1986), "Iran Arms Cash Tied to CIA-Run Account Aiding Afghan Rebels," *Washington Post*, December 3, 1986.

Shirin, Tahir-Kheli, (1982), The United States and Pakistan: The Evolution of an Influence Relationship, New York: Praeger.

Shriwashtava, B.K. (2000), "US tilt towards Pakistan" *World Focus*, June-July 2002.

SP Verma, Foreign Policy in South Asia, Jaipur 1969), p. 237.

Spector, Leonard S. (1985), *The New Nuclear Nations*, New York: Vintage Books.

The Pakistan-US Security relationship, Iftikhar H. Mallik, Asian Survey, Vol. xxx, No. 3 March 1990, p. 284.

Venkatramani, M.S. (1982), *American Role in Pakistan*, New Delhi.

Verma, SP (1969), Foreign Policy in South Asia, Jaipur.

Chapter 2

Responding to Afghanistan Crisis

The most important foreign policy challenge for the US at the time of Ronald Reagan's entry into the White House was the Soviet invasion of Afghanistan. In the nineteenth century, Afghanistan served as a strategic buffer state between Czarist Russia and the British Empire in the subcontinent. Afghanistan's relations with Moscow became more cordial after the Bolshevik Revolution in 1917. The Soviet Union was the first country to establish diplomatic relations with Afghanistan after the Third Anglo-Afghan war and signed an Afghan-Soviet non-aggression pact in 1921, which also provided for Afghan transit rights through the Soviet Union. Early Soviet assistance included financial aid, aircraft and attendant technical personnel, and telegraph operators.

The Soviets began a major economic assistance programme for Afghanistan in 1950s. Between 1954 and 1978, Afghanistan received more than $1 billion of Soviet aid. Moscow, also promised substantial military assistance to Kabul in 1973, along with the assistance related to gas and oil development, trade, transport, irrigation, and factory construction. Following the 1979 invasion, the Soviets augmented their large aid commitments to shore up the Afghan economy and rebuild the Afghan military. They provided the Karmal regime an unprecedented $800 million during the occupation (http://en.wikipedia.org/wiki/Foreign_relations_of_Afghanistan)

United States-Afghanistan relations can be traced back to over 150 years, to the early 1800s, when the first American, Josiah Harlan, and adventurer from Pennsylvania and adviser on Afghan politics, visited Afghanistan. In the 1940s, the United States established its first ever embassy in Kabul. The first American ambassador to Afghanistan was Cornelius Van Engert. The first US President to visit Afghanistan was Dwight Eisenhower, who travelled to Kabul in the 1950s, where he met the then King of Afghanistan, Zahir Shah. Closer relations between the United States and Afghanistan began to develop since then. In the 1830s, this reputedly inspired Rudyard Kipling's story "The Man Who Would Be King".

In 1942, Major Gordon Enders of the US Army was appointed "the first military attache to the non-existent US embassy in Kabul. He was the first envoy of any kind to be sent to represent the United States in Kabul." During the 1950s and 1979s, US provided foreign assistance to Afghanistan worth more than $500 million in loans, grants, and surplus agricultural commodities to develop transportation facilities, increase agricultural production, expand the educational system, stimulate industry, and improve government administration. In the 1950s, the US declined Afghanistan's request for defence cooperation but extended an economic assistance programme focused on the development of Afghanistan's physical infrastructure- roads, dams, and power plants. Later, the US aid shifted from infrastructure projects to technical assistance programmes to help develop the skills needed to build a modern economy. The US Peace Corps was also active in Afghanistan between 1962 and 1979. During the early 1960s, former King of Afghanistan, Zahir Shah, visited the United States and met John F. Kennedy at the White House in Washington, DC. After the April 1978 coup, US-Afghan relations deteriorated. In February 1979, US Ambassador Adolph "Spike" Dubs was murdered in Kabul. The US then reduced bilateral assistance and terminated a small military training programme. All remaining assistance agreements were ended after the Soviet invasion in December 1979. Following the Soviet invasion, the

United States first supported vigours diplomatic efforts to achieve a Soviet withdrawal. In addition, generous US contributions to the refugee programme in Pakistan played a major part in efforts to assist Afghans in need. US efforts also included helping Afghans living inside Afghanistan. This cross-border humani-tarian assistance programme aimed at increasing Afghan self- sufficiency and helping Afghans resist Soviet attempts to drive civilians out of the rebeldominated countryside. (http://en.wikipedia.org/wiki/US-Afghanistan_relations)

Before the Soviet invasion, Afghanistan pursued a policy of neutrality and nonalignment in its foreign relations, being one of a few independent nations to stay neutral in both World War I and World War II. In international forums, Afghanistan generally followed the voting patterns of Asian and African non-aligned countries. During the 1950s and 60s, Afghanistan was able to receive economic assistance from both the super-powers. However, given that unlike Russia, America refused to give extensive military aid to the country, the government of Mohammed Daoud Khan developed warmer ties with the USSR while officially remaining nonaligned. Following the Marxist coup of April 1978, the Taraki government developed significantly closer ties with the Soviet Union and its communist satellites. After the December 1979 invasion, Afghanistan's foreign policy mirrored that of the Soviet Union. Afghan foreign policy-makers attempted, with little success, to increase their regime's low standing in the non-communist world. Most Western countries, including the United States, maintained small diplomatic missions in the capital city of Kabul during the Soviet occupation. Many countries subsequently closed their missions due to instability and heavy fighting in Kabul after the Soviet withdrawal in 1989. The areas of Nuclear Weapon Free Zone (NWFZ) and Balochistan-have long complicated Afghanistan's relations with Pakistan. Contro-versies involving these areas date back to the establishment of the Durand Line in 1893 dividing Pashtun and Baluch tribes living in Afghanistan from those living in what later became Pakistan. Afghanistan vigorously protested the inclusion of Pashtun and Baluch areas within Pakistan without providing the inhabitants with an opportunity for self-determination. Since the birth of Pakistan in 1947, there have been problems concerning incidents along the border, with extensive disruption of normal trade patterns. One of the most serious crisis lasted from September 1961 to June 1963, when diplomatic, trade, transit, and consular relations between the countries were suspended.

The 1978 Marxist coup further strained relations between the two countries. Pakistan took the lead diplomatically in the United Nations, the Non-Aligned Movement, and the Organisation of the Islamic Conference in opposing the Soviet occupation. During the war against the Soviet occupation, Pakistan served as the primary logistical conduit for the Afghan resistance. Pakistan, aided by UN agencies, private groups, and many friendly countries, continued to provide refuge to several million Afghans. (http://en.wikipedia.org/wiki/Foreign_relations_of_Afghanistan). Soon after the Soviet invasion, the US State Department warned the Soviet combat troop's intervention in Afghanistan and alleged that it created severe security problems for Pakistan (New York Times, December 23, 1979.

According to the reports, the US looked then for China's cooperation to boost Pakistan's defence policy against Soviet military pressure. An American official said that joint plan might be developed to increase arms aid to Pakistan and stop the crisis in Afghanistan (New York Times, January 3, 1980). US Secretary, Harold Brown, however, indicated that no agreement had been reached with China on coordinating Chinese and American military aid to Pakistan in the wake of Soviet intervention in Afghanistan. (New York Times, January 10, 1980) The Soviet Union, on the other hand, alleged that President Carter's main purpose in seeking resumption of large-scale arms shipments to Pakistan was to get weapons into the hands of Afghan rebels (New York Times, January 5, 1980). Presidential aspirant Ronald Reagan stated in a press conference that he supported 'funneling' American arms to forces in Afghanistan, so that Pakistan could then tranship to Afghan forces in 'signal' to Russians that America had deep concern about intervention. (New York Times, January 11, 1980). President Carter and Secretary of State Cyrus R Vance in the mean time met with Pakistan's Foreign Minister Agha Shahi in Washington and reaffirm which US commitment to territorial integrity and security of Pakistan; in response to Soviet intervention in Afghanistan, (New York Times, January 13, 1980).

While Pakistani military forces were the largest and most experienced in Southwest Asian and Persian Gulf region, they were in-short supply of modern weapons. Washington then decided to arm Pakistan (New York Times, January 14, 1980).

Henry A Kissinger suggested that US consider establishment of air and naval bases in Pakistan to wards off possible Soviet threat. (*ibid*)

Some analysts argued that arming of Pakistan could harm Indo-US relations, the New York Times in its editorial said that was India concerned that a Pakistan aligned with China, financed by Moslem wealth, armed by US and perhaps bolstered by capacity to produce nuclear weapons might one day attack India to avenge loss Bangladesh and suggested that that US must take such concern into account in formulating policy on Pakistan (New York Times, January 15, 1980). Pakistan President General Mohammed Zia-ul-Haq in the mean time appealed strongly for international aid and support in face of what Pakistan regarded as a grave threat posed by Soviet invasion of Afghanistan. He hoped US decision to provide Pakistan with 400 million in aid would be 'without strings'; but other high-ranking Pakistan Government officials said privately that US offer was inadequate. (New York Times, January 16, 1980). President Carter, in State of Union Message, expressed concern that Soviet intervention in Afghanistan might worsen the situation for Pakistan; keeping this in view, he decided to ask Congress to reaffirm 1959 commitment to provide military and economic aid to Pakistan; (New York Times, January 24, 1980).

When Reagan became the US President, his officials soon clarified that effort would be made to include Pakistan in proposed increased programme of military assistance to some countries because of direct threat posed to that nation by Soviet troops in Afghanistan (New York Times, March 8, 1981). US Attorney General Edwin Meese arrived in Islamabad, Pakistan, on a two-day visit to show US support for Pakistan's policy toward Afghanistan and its fight against drugs (New York Times, March 24, 1986). Pakistan President Mohammad Zia-ul-Haq was not approved to the US to mounting idea of occasional patrols in Pakistani airspace with early warning aircraft that could detect attacks coming from Afghanistan; illustration (New York Times, October 16, 1986). Defence Secretary Casper Weinberger said that US would seek to provide early warning radar planes to Pakistan as quickly possible to help defend against incursions from Afghanistan (New York Times, October 17, 1986). A close security relationship with Pakistan has been the cornerstone of US policy in South Asia for more than three decades. Beginning with the Eisenhower administration, Washington regarded that Pakistan, together with Iran, could be an essential obstacle to Soviet expansionism towards the Indian Ocean and the oil fields of the Persian Gulf. Following the Iranian revolution and the Soviet invasion of Afghanistan in 1979, Pakistan acquired an even greater importance as a component of US geopolitical strategy throughout that region.

The strategic cooperation between Washington and Islamabad was first symbolised by a security agreement concluded in 1959, and the relationship became far more comprehensive. The United States has provided more than five billion dollars in economic and military aid to Islamabad since the mid-1950s. Pakistan's armed forces, 12th largest in the world, were equipped with an array of modern weapons, courtesy of the American treasury. A succession of governments in Islamabad rewarded this US generosity by consistently supporting US foreign policy positions,a marked contrast to the stance adopted by most Third World states. (Shirin, Tahir-Kheli, 1982, pp. 11-12).

The US-Pakistan connection survived a host of difficulties. India's supporters in the United States contended that support for Pakistan needlessly drove a wedge between this country and the world's most populous democracy. Such critics repeatedly advised American officials to recognise that India was the dominant power on the subcontinent and desired that US policy be adjusted to reflect that reality. While this view attracted several prestigious adherents over the years, including John Kenneth Galbraith, Chester Bowles, and at least during his Senate career, John F. Kennedy, its impact on US policy was limited. Pressure from pro-India forces did impel President Lyndon Johnson to embargo arms aid to Pakistan during the 1965 Indo-Pakistan conflict, when it became evident that Pakistan had violated restrictions on the assistance by using US supplied weapons for aggressive purposes. Similar lobbying contributed to a decision by the Carter administration to suspend economic and military assistance because of Pakistan's surreptitious military nuclear programme. But the basic features of a close US-Pakistan relationship survived such setbacks. A succession of American administrations stressed the importance of political and military ties with Islamabad even when this position severely strained relations with New Delhi and contributed to growing Indo-Soviet cooperation. Endemic political instability in Pakistan also strained its relations with Washington. The 1971 "tilt" occurred in the aftermath of a bloody civil war in which East Pakistan broke away to form the new nation of Bangladesh. During the mid-1970s, the government in Islamabad fought a lengthy and difficult campaign to suppress another separatist movement in Baluchistan province. Other secessionist impulses, while less potent, surfaced repeatedly throughout the country's troubled history. A continuing source of alarm for the United States was Pakistan's apparent determination to develop a military nuclear capability to match a similar programme in India. Not only did this strategy undermine Washington's long-standing effort to prevent the proliferation of nuclear weapons, it created undesirable risks for the United States.

American policy-makers exhibited considerable uneasiness about Pakistan obtaining nuclear armaments given that country's exceedingly hostile relationship with India. Such ominous developments should have caused US policy-makers to reconsider the wisdom of investing so much diplomatic, political, and military capital in an unpredictable and unstable ally. For a brief period during the early years of the Carter administration there was some evidence of a re- evaluation, but any inclination to deemphasise the Pakistan connection vanished when Soviet troops invaded Afghanistan. The Carter administration promptly muted its criticism of the Zia regime's human rights record, reiterated the 1959 security guarantee, and offered a new package of military aid totalling some $400 million.

During the intervening years, Pakistan resumed its traditional role as America's principal political and military outpost in South Asia. Congress authorised a $3.2 billion five-year aid package in 1981, and the Reagan administration requested a new programme exceeding $4 billion when the original measure expired at the end of FY 1987. In exchange, Washington pressured the Zia government to serve as a conduit for covert US military aid to Afghan rebel forces, the Mujaheddin, fighting the Soviet occupation army. That assistance by mid-eighties was estimated at $250-$300 million annually. (Omang, Joanne, *Washington Post*, October 10, 1985). The direct aid to Pakistan (which included F-16 fighters and other sophisticated weapons in the American arsenal normally not available to Third World allies) combined with Islamabad's heightened role in the Afghanistan conflict underscored how much the United States invested in its South Asian policy. Evidence suggests, however, that it is a risky and unwise commitment.

Washington viewed Pakistan both as a bulwark in its own right against Soviet expansion, and as an important component of American policy towards South and Southwest Asia. But Pakistan proved to be an extraordinarily frail ally–an impoverished nation with a history of political separatism and instability, governed precariously by military strongmen in the face of mounting domestic opposition. The last point was underscored in April 1986 when massive anti-government crowds greeted the return from exile of Benazir Bhutto, daughter of the country's last elected prime minister and heir to his political machine. Pakistan seemed destined for yet another period of acrimonious confrontation and domestic turmoil. By placing so much reliance on a weak and unstable ally, the United States risked the collapse of its entire South Asian policy. For a time, this confrontational strategy seemed to work. It gradually became evident; however, that Benazir Bhutto overestimated both the breadth of public dissatisfaction with the Zia regime and the depth of allegiance to her. Calls for massive demonstrations in July on the ninth anniversary of Zia's coup against her father resulted in disappointing turnouts. Ignoring this warning that she might be overreaching herself, Bhutto and her organisation again took to the streets the following month. This time there were continuous, sizable demonstrations in her home province of Sind, but elsewhere the initial outpouring of support quickly evaporated. Moreover, the government of Zia's hand-picked Prime Minister, Mohammad Khan Junejo, responded to the provocations by declaring a state of emergency and jailing Bhutto and hundreds of her followers. This crackdown marked a reversal of hesitant but encouraging steps towards democracy, including the election of a "non-partisan" parliament in 1985 and the legalisation of political parties in early 1986.

Benazir Bhutto had openly tried to duplicate the successful revolution led by Corazon Aquino in the Philippines. It was an image she evoked in most of her speeches, and the Western news media were quick to proclaim "parallels" between the Philippine and Pakistan struggles. (Newsweek, July 7, 1986, pp. 33-35), But by the autumn of 1986, one extremely clear difference had emerged: While Aquino had swept into office amid the acclaim of a decisive majority of her countrymen; Bhutto failed in her initial bid for power. The divergent results should not have been so surprising to Western observers. So-called parallels with the revolution in the Philippines were vastly overdrawn. While some similarities existed, there were also crucial differences. The United States could not have expected a bloodless transfer of power to a democratic, pro-Western government. Pakistan's history and the dynamics of the current political environment suggested a less appealing outcome. Indeed, the personalised struggle between President Zia and his challenger often obscured more fundamental problems that, quite literally, threatened to unravel Pakistan as a nation-state. It was this latter possibility that posed a lethal danger to the US policy in the region.

The Baghdad Pact suffered a severe blow almost immediately when Iraq withdrew following an anti-Western revolution in 1958. Turkey increasingly gravitated towards its association with Western Europe through NATO, showing only modest interest in South Asian problems. The United States moved quickly to fill at least part of the void through bilateral arrangements with both Pakistan and Iran, but that approach also collapsed following the 1979 Iranian revolution. Only Pakistan remained to fulfil its assigned role as a US-sponsored guard in South Asia, when the Soviet invaded in Afghanistan. From the American perspective, the most direct danger to Pakistan arising from its status as America's military client was an increased Soviet and Indian hostility. India expectedly resented US military assistance to its arch-rival, Pakistan. New Delhi regarded the arrangement during the Soviet intervention both as an unwarranted American intrusion into what was rightfully India's geographic sphere of influence, and as a direct threat to its national security. The Reagan administration's decision to give Pakistan advanced weaponry, including 40 F-16 fighters, especially angered the Indira Gandhi government. While the United States insisted that this assistance was designed to bolster Pakistan's ability to defend itself from possible Soviet aggression, India could hardly. Clearly, the Pakistani arsenal could be used against India in some future conflict.

US military aid thus heightened Indian hostility towards Pakistan and became irritant Indo-American relations as well.

(Frankel, Francine R., 1986, pp. 148-166). US arms transfer to Pakistan gave India and the Soviet Union a common focal point for their foreign policy concerns, thus helping to cement an otherwise curious partnership between a democracy and the world's most powerful totalitarian state. Its role as a US military and political outpost in South Asia placed Pakistan on the frontlines in an ongoing superpower struggle. This caused the Kremlin to pay an inordinate amount of attention to an otherwise relatively neglected Third World country like India. Some US analysts felt that Moscow had an obvious incentive to eliminate US influence on its geopolitical doorstep, either through military intimidation or attempts at destabilisation". Pakistan's manifest internal weaknesses gave the Soviets "ample opportunity for mischief," especially in the area of subversion. The Soviets allegedly cultivated extensive contacts with Baluchistan's separatist leaders for many years and apparently provided modest clandestine aid to the rebels during the uprising in the 1970s. There were also indications that Moscow maintained contact with "left-wing elements" in the anti-Zia coalition. While such subversive activities remained at relatively low levels, potential for a more concerted campaign existed. Using Pakistan as the principal conduit for US military assistance to the Afghan Mujaheddin exposed that nation to grave risks. The USSR obviously regarded Afghanistan as a high-priority foreign policy concern. Moscow would scarcely have had destroyed detente with the United States and committed 120,000 troops to a seemingly endless war if this were not the case. Therefore, the Kremlin leaders likely regarded joint US-Pakistani assistance to the Afghan rebels as a serious challenge to Soviet interests. The Red Army's difficulty in crushing the insurgency and restore stability to Afghanistan on Moscow's terms created an additional incentive to strike directly at Pakistan without risking a global conflagration, through a strategy to increase political and military pressure on the more vulnerable antagonist-Pakistan.

Some observer feared that while the obvious and most probable threat to Pakistan came in the form of heightened Soviet subversion activities, an even more ominous danger existed. If the Afghan stalemate continued, and especially if the Mujaheddin seemed poised to topple the Kabul regime despite Soviet military assistance, Moscow could be tempted to strike directly at the sanctuaries across the border in Pakistan. There had already been dozens of "minor" incidents, primarily crossborder shelling and intrusions into Pakistani air space by Soviet and Afghan planes (Military Review, March 1986, pp. 68-75). As time passed and Afghan insurgency proved a hard nut, Soviet protests to Islamabad concerning the use of Pakistani territory as sanctuaries by the Mujaheddin noticeably become more strident. It was feared that Should Moscow attempt to wipe out those sanctuaries or even adopt a limited "hot pursuit" policy-it would create an extremely grave situation. The Zia government would face an unpalatable choice. If it failed to respond to such blatant provocations, the government would be tacitly conceding an inability to defend the homeland. Given the Zia regime's already precarious position, such a humiliation might well topple it from power. Yet, a military response would involve the risk of a perilous confrontation with the USSR-one difficult to contain. The possibility of Soviet military pressure on Pakistan posed serious risks to the United States as well as for Pakistan.

The ongoing political and military association with Pakistan endangered American security in three ways. A Soviet move against the Afghan border sanctuaries would probably impel Islamabad to invoke the 1959 security pact, since it was extremely unlikely that the Pakistanis would take on the Red Army alone. In addition, Washington had also strengthened its commitment following the invasion of Afghanistan by proclaiming the Carter Doctrine, pledging resistance to any further Soviet aggression towards the Persian Gulf-Indian Ocean region. US officials would, therefore, have had to decide whether to dishonour those commitments or come to the aid of Pakistan even though it entailed a probable direct confrontation with the USSR.

The American dilemma was reflected in the fact that it was uncertain how effective American assistance might be, given the inherent geographic limitations of the region. While the United States maintained a significant naval presence in the Indian Ocean, including a rapid deployment force, American military presence would be dwarfed by those of the USSR. The Soviets would be operating less than 1,000 miles away from their homeland; the United States more than 8,000. The 1959 security treaty was created at a time when the United States enjoyed a decisive edge over the USSR in nuclear weaponry. Could Washington threaten a devastating response, if Moscow dared attack Pakistan at a time of nuclear parity? Would the US policy-makers risk a nuclear war to fight communism in a backward, Third World and landlocked country? Would Reagan administration be able to convince the US Congress and the American people the need to fight a nuclear war with the Soviet Union? If met, what could the Reagan Administration do to protest its ally?

The United States connection with Islamabad raised another risk. While the US- Pak security treaty applied explicitly to communist aggression, the close association between India and the USSR made that point ambiguous. The Zia government openly accused India of being an undeclared Soviet ally and could well argue that an attack from that quarter constituted a Soviet-orchestrated threat. It should be noted that the government of Pakistan attempted a similar ploy in the 1971 war, at a time when Indo-Soviet cooperation was considerably less extensive (*Washington Quarterly*, Spring- 1986, pp. 109-122). Some US analysts drew attention to the danger of an Indo-US conflict, if Pakistan employed its modern American-made weapons in the event of an Indo-Pak war. The United States would face a terrible dilemma, if the war particularly went badly for Pakistan. Unless Indian objectives remained extremely limited, there would exist considerable pressure on American officials to prevent that outcome, even if it meant risking a military clash with India. It is indicative of the tension on this score between New Delhi and Washington that Indian public opinion increasingly regarded a military conflict with the United States as a serious possibility. The possible consequences of American involvement in a new war between Pakistan and India must be, according to US analysts, assessed against the backdrop of nuclear weapons development in both countries. India demonstrated its capability by detonating an atomic device in 1974, and rumors abounded that New Delhi now possessed a small arsenal. The Zia government insisted officially that Pakistan had no nuclear weapons programme, but this had no credibility either inside or outside the country. (*Washington Post*, November 5, 1986)

The American debate also focused on yet another serious risk. Washington had built an elaborate geopolitical strategy in South Asia, assuming an obligation to keep the Persian Gulf oil routes open and escalating assistance to the rebels in Afghanistan. Crucial to this regional policy was the continuation of Pakistan as an effective political and military ally. The loss of Pakistan, either through external pressure or domestic turmoil, could literally destroy the edifice of American strategy in South Asia. By basing its strategy so totally on a weak and unstable ally, the United States risked creating regional chaos and probably an irresistible opportunity for Soviet expansionism precisely what Washington struggled to prevent for decades. Same argued that the preservation of a stable, non-communist barrier to Soviet expansion in South Asia required US military disengagement from the region and an end to the Pakistani connection. In the mean time, Pakistan also began to recognise some of the dangers involved in being America's client. Despite receiving millions of dollars per year in US economic and military aid, the Zia government was increasingly resisting US demands related to policy towards Afghanistan. Pakistan was not entirely comfortable in its role as conduit for American military aid to the Mujahidin. Afghan rebel leaders often complained for years that equipment destined for their forces was delayed or even siphoned off by Pakistani officials. There were also loud objections that sophisticated weapons such as the shoulder launched "Stinger" ground-to-air missiles were being intercepted. (*Washington Post*, January 16, 1986)

The Zia regime, morever, feared that channelling military aid to the Mujahidin risked antagonising the Soviet Union, bringing about more border incidents and an increase in other nonetoo- subtle Soviet pressures. Moreover, Pakistan's leaders were nervous about arming powerful Mujahidin units which they could hardly control. President Zia served as an official attached to the embassy in Jordan in 1969 and 1970, when King Hussein found his power severely eroded by the PLO, and this experience had apparently made an indelible impression on him. Zia knew how perilous it could be to his political fortunes to have a well-armed foreign guerrilla army operating in his country with little control over this non-state actor. Despite intense US pressure to assist the Mujahidin and the pull of religious solidarity, the Zia government passing green regarded its role with mounting apprehension.

The divergence of Pakistani and US objectives was similarly evident with respect to diplomatic positions concerning Afghanistan. For example, Washington was doubtful about the effectiveness of the UN-sponsored negotiations to end the Afghan conflict. It demanded a prompt and total withdrawal of Soviet forces with little consideration for the subsequent survival of the Kabul regime. In short, US leaders sought Soviet concessions that would either guarantee a Mujahidin victory or at least create a predominantly non-communist successor government in Kabul. While officially endorsing the UN talks, American officials considered them as little more than "a snare" designed to achieve what the USSR was unable to attain on the battlefield recognition of its quisling regime and contribution of a modest Soviet military presence in Afghanistan.

Islamabad did not share the US perception and adopted a somewhat different view. It remained an active participant in UN-sponsored negotiations since their inception in 1982. While Islamabad demanded a definite time-table for the withdrawal of Soviet troops, it also displayed a willingness to discuss various compromise measures. In marked contrast to the US insistence that the Mujahidin be a party to negotiations for a settlement of the Afghan conflict, Pakistan appeared to be more interested in direct talks between Islamabad and Kabul assuming that the Soviet troop withdrawal would take place.

These disagreements constituted a significant source of tension between the United States and Pakistan.

Some Pakistanis also feared that the Reagan administration was using Afghanistan as a testing ground for the so-called Reagan Doctrine of providing aid to anti-Soviet insurgents in the Third World and use the Mujahidin to tie down Soviet military forces in a bloody and protracted conflict. The Pakistani government, moreover, was worried about the massive Afghan refugee presence in its country and the burden placed on an already fragile domestic, social and political structure. Pakistani officials perhaps had a much greater reason to seek a compromising solution, even if that must come at the expense of the insurgents. They desired a settlement, above all, that would eliminate the Soviet military threat to Pakistan's border and enable the Afghan refugees to go home.

If the Reagan administration found the Zia government to be an increasingly reluctant and recalcitrant ally, it was unlikely to be happy with a democratically elected government in Islamabad in the backdrop of the intense Cold War. The Pakistan People's Party (PPP) explicitly advocated a non-aligned foreign policy and condemned Zia for doing Washington's bidding in South Asia. Bhutto and her followers promised not to allow their country to be used as a sanctuary for the Afghan insurgents or make the country a distribution hub for US arms destined for the Mujahidin. A significant faction within other principal opposition group, the MRD, was even more virulently anti-American, routinely denouncing the Zia regime as an instrument of "US imperialism". Given the growing public concern about the presence of the Afghan refugees and danger of a military clash with the USSR, the anti-Zia forces tried to capitalise on this. Zia regime's cautious but visible attempts to distance itself from the more doctrinaire aspects of the US policy, on the other hand, caused worries in Washington about the reliability of Pakistan as an ally. (*Ibid*). Critics pointed out that Washington's strategy of using client states as a base of operations in the region in order to minimize the Soviet advantage was doomed to failure. Pakistan was the last of those clients, and the burden of U.S. demands threatened to become a catalyst plunging that nation into disaster. If American policy-makers truly believed that a stable, non- communist Pakistan constituted an essential barrier to Soviet expansionism, then a drastic reorientation of US policy was essential.

Pakistan was already weak with a non-democratic regime and backward economy. The Afghan crisis accentuated Pakistan's problems. A more hospitable external environment would greatly facilitate Pakistan's ability to institute political and economic reforms. One crucial feature of that environment was diminished Soviet and Indian hostility, but such a change was unlikely to occur so long as Pakistan remained a political and military client of the US. On the contrary, pressure from Moscow and New Delhi was unlikely to go if the USSR pursued an elusive victory in Afghanistan and India complained about having a neighbour armed with nuclear weapons serving as a surrogate for American power. One school of analysts pointed out that US relations with Pakistan was more a reward to the Pakistani military than to the country. The vast quantities of American military aid since the 1950s had greatly strengthened the Pakistani military at the expense of the civilian sector. This in turn weakened further fragile democratic structure of the country and distorted Pakistan's economy, gearing it towards a garrison state. The Reagan Administration's uncritical support for the "friendly" autocratic government headed by Zia-ul-Haq antagonised competing political elements and strengthened separatist forces that saw no hope for change within Pakistan. Employing Pakistan as an instrument for carrying out US policy in Afghanistan thus created more political and social instability (ibid).

The Reagan Administration was not in a position to contemplate military disengagement from the region. The Soviets might just regard US disengagement as an opportunity to embark on further expansionist binge throughout the region, either by accelerating the subversion of neighbouring states or by direct aggression. In this worst case scenario, Pakistan could very well be the first victim on Moscow's expansionist menu.

There were also worries in certain American quarters that the US disengagement could encourage Indian hegemonic aspirations. The "religious animosity", the territorial dispute involving Kashmir, and mutual suspicions concerning rival nuclear weapons programmes could "ignite a fourth Indo-Pak war", and without American military commitment a decisive Indian victory would be almost certain.

However, there was no agreement on such assessment. It was argued that while some danger existed that Moscow or New Delhi might respond to a US military withdrawal from South Asia by crushing Pakistan, there was ample reason to expect a more peaceful aftermath. The Soviets in particular would pay an exceedingly high price if they moved to establish their power on the shores of the Indian Ocean. The USSR could not expect India to support its policy of expansionism. A discernible cooling of Indo-Soviet relations had already taken place as the Soviet occupation of Afghanistan dragged on. It was extremely doubtful if the Indira Gandhi government would regard a Soviet-controlled Pakistan on India's border as anything but a menace to its national security. In short, the USSR could achieve its coveted warm water ports only at grave risk to its relationship with India, an association Moscow considered vital to counter Chinese power. It was unlikely that the Kremlin leaders would be willing to pay such an exorbitant price. Pakistan, therefore, represented an important buffer between Soviet and Indian spheres of influence.

Yet another school of analysts found Pakistan to be a hopeless case. According to them, even if Pakistan avoided external calamities, severe internal political and economic difficulties would continue in the struggle between conservative forces supporting the government and the coalition of moderate and radical opposition elements. The Sind-Punjab rivalry and the separatist campaigns in Baluchistan were unlikely to end soon. Thus, even under the best of circumstances, Pakistan's continued survival would remain a question mark. (*Ibid*). However, the situation was neither overtly optimistic nor completely hopeless. There were subtle signs that Moscow was becoming weary of its military involvement in Afghanistan. General Secretary Mikhail Gorbachev acknowledged that Afghanistan was becoming "a bleeding wound". At the same time, Moscow refused to withdraw from that country in a manner that would give the United States a major geopolitical victory.

According to an analyst, US policy-makers had the opportunity to offer the Soviet Union an extremely tempting package deal. The arrangement would involve an "Austrian solution" to both Afghanistan and Pakistan. Essential features of such an accord would include:

- A complete Soviet military withdrawal from Afghanistan and the formation of a new government in Kabul, including representatives of the Mujahidin;
- A termination of the security agreement between the United States and Pakistan;
- A commitment from both superpowers that they will provide no military assistance to any faction in Afghanistan or Pakistan;
- A stipulation among all parties that neither Afghanistan nor Pakistan will join any bilateral or multilateral military arrangement with either superpower; and
- A guarantee by the USSR and India to respect the independence and territorial integrity of Afghanistan and Pakistan.

Nuclear Proliferation

For a number of reasons, US non-proliferation legislation and the Administration's diplomatic efforts have tended to focus primarily on Pakistan, rather than India or China, the latter of which is already recognised as a legitimate nuclear weapons state under the NPT. The lack of "symmetry" in the treatment of India and Pakistan that is now being criticised by Pakistan and some in Congress was never a deliberate policy decision, however. Rather, US non-proliferation policies towards both countries arose out of special historical circumstances and practical considerations. Among other things, US non-proliferation legislation has focused on the *transfer* of nuclear materials and technology, not their indigenous development. It is widely acknowledged that this approach was adopted in part to avoid having Israel fall under the scope of non-proliferation based aid restrictions. Coincidentally, this also benefited India, which, like Israel, has an indigenous capability for developing nuclear weapons.

The United States has not ignored India's nuclear activities, however. India's 1974 nuclear test served as a major spur to the passage of the Nuclear Non-Proliferation Act of 1978. As a result of the passage of that legislation, the United States eventually abrogated a 1963 nuclear cooperation agreement that otherwise committed it for 30 years to make commercial sales of enriched uranium for India's US-built nuclear power station at Tarapur, near Bombay, due to India's refusal to put all of its nuclear facilities under international inspection. However, India had already tested a nuclear device before the adoption of the sections of the foreign assistance act that sought to check Pakistan's drive to acquire nuclear weapons. Security is basically a relational phenomenon and an ambiguous concept (Wolfers, 1962, p. 10). It is a broader idea than power, and it has the useful feature of incorporating much of the insight, which derives from the analysis of power. (Buzan, http://jpr.sagepub.com/cgi/content/refs/21/2/109).

In his theory of international politics, Kenneth Waltz identifies that states can balance against threats. States can balance externally, through alliances, or internally, through military preparations. (Waltz, 1979, p. 168.) Both types of balancing incur costs; alliances bring commitments and the threat of unwanted entanglement, while military preparations divert scarce resources from other important projects. In the modern world, states operate in a "self-defence" system in which threats to national security are omnipresent. Most of the 'weak' and 'small' states, in particular, have difficulties in meeting the challenges from powerful neighbours, since such states are by definition limited in their ability to build sizeable and well-equipped military machines.(Handel, 1981, pp. 56-76). In other words, strong states with mature institutions, well-defined territories and strong national identities may well promote the security of their people and be able to counter any external threat. (Sorensen, *Security Dialogue*, p. 377). In contemporary times, the ultimate balance is nuclear weapons. States can either seek nuclear guarantees from established nuclear powers, or they can construct their own nuclear weapons. In this regard, Michael Handel analyses the place of weak states in the international system, claiming that a few small states reconcile themselves to "defensive nihilism", the abandonment of hope to establish an effective defence (Handel, 1981, p. 77). Waltz believes that "the gradual spread of nuclear weapons will promote peace and reinforce international stability because nuclear weapons induce caution between adversaries who possess them or more may be better" (Waltz, 1981, p. 30). Nuclear weapons are incomparably more devastating than conventional military power. They reduce the probability of a major global war because nuclear weapons are not vulnerable. Moreover, nuclear weapons can make it possible to compress the fury of war without the collapse of the state. They can change the speed, control and the sequence of events and can provide protection from the threat of military defeat and total destruction (Thayer, *Security Studies,* 1995, pp. 150-155). Hans Morgenthau has observed that nuclear weapons can reduce the conventional threats posed by adversaries and increase state's security in an anarchic world. (Morgenthau, *American Political Science Review*, 1964, p. 35). In the Third World countries, which are traditional enemies, and in close proximity, mutual disputes and conflicts are endemic and quickly come to engage critical interests. One strategist contends, "Leaders of the Third World may be ready to risk nuclear confrontation, irrespective of high levels of nuclear damage, in pursuit of their national interest or objectives." (Kaiser, 1989, pp. 123-136.). Of the gravest concern is the fear that inter-state conflict in Third World states will also socialise states so that they consider military force, even nuclear weapons, in terms of waging war, rather than in terms of deterrence. It seems equally clear that defensively minded states cannot compete against powerful states and only nuclear weapons can provide a strong guarantee that a state will not be put in a position of losing everything, even at the hands of an aggressor, which also has nuclear weapons.

The birth of Pakistan's nuclear programme was in direct response to its defeat in the Bangladesh War in 1971 and after India's nuclear test in 1974. These two events provided Pakistan with evidence of its insecurity in regard to both its sovereignty and its inability to deter possible Indian aggression. Nuclear weapons were seen as an "equaliser", making up for Pakistan's lack of strategic depth and conventional asymmetry. Pakistan's development of the nuclear option is the result, at least in part, of its lack of success in its competition with India (Hoyt, 2005, pp. 113-115). Accordingly, nuclear weapons have always formed the centre-piece in Pakistan's search for "strategic equality" with India, which has deep historical roots stretching back to the partition of the two countries in 1947. The relations between United States have the two main key issues: developing aid policy and another Pakistan's nuclear policy. On the first, it argues that the Soviet withdrawal from Afghanistan, plus US budget constraints, indicate that "extraordinarily high levels of aid cannot and should not be maintained". On the second, it asserts that the USA should, if it proves unable to persuade Pakistan to renounce its nuclear programme, lower its sights and settle for Pakistani agreement not to test nuclear weapons. After a period of more than a decade during which Afghanistan dominated the political situation in South Asia, the withdrawal of Soviet forces has significantly altered the political situation within the region. India and Pakistan face new realities, and outside powers will also need to readjust their policies to take account of the changing issues in the region.

The Soviet involvement in Afghanistan drew the United States into a much more active role in South Asia than it had played for over a decade; a restored US relationship with Pakistan was the principal channel. In Afghanistan, the United States achieved a signal policy success; the determination of both the Carter and Reagan administrations to back the Afghan resistance forces has paid off beyond all expectations. The restoration of democratic rule in Pakistan is also something in which Americans can take satisfaction. Although the overwhelming credit belongs to the Pakistani people (just as the success in Afghanistan belongs largely to Afghans), the United States played a more than marginal role by making clear its preference for the restoration of democracy. Like most foreign policy successes, these two develop-mints have spawned new problems. The United States must consider how to react to the Soviet withdrawal from Afghanistan: Should they use this favourable situation to enhance our role in the region along the Soviets' southern flank? Or should the United States reduce its heavy commitment in such a distant region and postpone thinking about South Asia until more pressing problems elsewhere have been taken in hand? Similarly, the US relationship with Pakistan needs reshaping. The Soviet withdrawal from Afghanistan reduces the need for an intimate relationship with Islamabad, but we must decide just what kind of bilateral relationship we want and how Pakistan may fit into whatever broader strategy we choose. The return of democratic government in Pakistan roughly compensates for what would have been a post-Afghanistan decline in America's interest there and improves the context of our bilateral relations. But it does not fundamentally change some of the major bilateral issues-especially Pakistan's nuclear programme, the turbulent state of its politics, and the sheer size of the US aid programme in Pakistan. In the near term there are still other differences that remain to be dealt with, including our respective positions on the further evolution of events within Afghanistan. Pakistan should never be considered a negligible quantity in any geopolitical calculation. It ranks among the world's ten most populous nations; it has distinguished itself through adroit diplomacy; it has a large and competent military; it plays an important role in South Asia. (http://nuclear internet\U_S_-Pakistani nuclear Relations.htm)

In the beginning of the Cold War, Pakistan aligned itself with the United States by joining two regional defence pacts, the South East Asia Treaty Organisation and the Baghdad Pact. As a result of these alliances, Pakistan received nearly $2 billion in US assistance from 1953 until 1961, a quarter of this in military aid, thus making Pakistan one of America's most important security partners of the period, "the most allied ally." (Alan Kronstadt, *CRS Issue Brief for Congress*, March 6, 2006, p. 3). Pakistan's nuclear preparation and doctrine have been based on fairly clear and straightforward means to forge a credible deterrent to counter India. In pursuit of this aim, Pakistan has been forced to shift from a policy of external balancing to one of internal balancing. Throughout its history, Pakistan's foreign policy has been dominated by the determination to incorporate Kashmir into the republic; its security policy, in turn, has been formed by the perceived threat from India, defined in terms of Kashmir and the integration of the Pakistani state. Since 1970s, Pakistan has been engaged in a major nuclear programme to enhance its nuclear weapons capability as a deterrent against India's overwhelming conventional and nuclear superiority. Thus, strategically, Pakistan's nuclear programme is driven mainly by its perception of threat and security concerns about India, which it claims has not fully accepted the existence of Pakistan as an independent country. Pakistan has always been a weak and vulnerable country and it would face great difficulty in prevailing in a war against India -resources, both military and civilian, are too limited. Pakistan cannot expect to match India tank for tank or gun for gun because the numbers are too great. According to William Pfaff, India's intransigence on bilateral disputes and her nuclear superiority have made Pakistani leaders feel compelled to see nuclear weapons as a hedge, in order to stay in the game. (Pfaff, *International Herald Tribune*, 3 June 1998)

Pakistan launched its own nuclear weapons programme and they had continued to expand its ability to produce weapons-grade nuclear material free from International Atomic Energy Agency (IAEA) safeguards and continued to resort to clandestine nuclear trade to advance its nuclear programme. The Pakistani military and political elite as an important component in national power always regarded technology, and in its nuclear weapons it has always aspired to a high-tech edge over its rivals. As a result, the Pakistanis have high regard for smart weapons and technologically advanced support systems has intensified. Prime Minister Zulfikar Ali Bhutto once declared that "Pakistanis would rather eat grass or leaves, or even go hungry, but we will get one of our own, than surrender the nuclear option". (Chellaney, *Survival*, Vol. 35, No.3, autumn 1993, p. 122)

Pakistan's nuclear policy was founded in the 1950s and the US "Atomic for Peace" programme trained Pakistani scientists in nuclear-reactor technology. They also enabled Pakistan to buy a 5 MW swimming pool type research reactor and fuel, too small to have any military significance, which became fully operational in 1965; it has been used mainly for training purposes. A Canadian 137 MW heavy-water type power plant reactor (KANUPP) was supplied on a turnkey basis and became operational in 1972. The KANUPP facility is a natural uranium, heavy water reactor of the CANDU type which, according to some sources, can produce as much as 55 kg of plutonium per year (4-6 bomb's worth) when operating at peak capacity. (Leventhal, *ORBIS*, spring 1992, p. 171.) However, the reactor has never operated at full capacity and since 1977, it has been operating at a sharply reduced level due to a cut-off in Canadian fuel supplies. Pakistan solicited bids for construction of a 900 MW light water, low enriched uranium fuelled power plant on the Indus River at Chashma, where it can draw on hydroelectric power with the co-operation of China. Zulfikar Ali Bhutto who provided a new direction to Pakistan's nuclear policy in the 1960s, as Minister for Natural Resources and Atomic Energy and later as a Foreign Minister had demonstrated keen interest in nuclear weapons. Quite appropriately, an Indian scholar, Ashok Kapur, has stated that Bhutto "mobilised nuclear nationalism in Pakistan" (Kapur, 1987, p. 58).

He declared in 1966 that if India built a nuclear bomb, Pakistan would follow suit, to retain a strategic balance with India, including the development of nuclear weapons, at any cost. In 1969, Bhutto wrote: "All wars of our age have become total wars...It would be dangerous to plan for less, and our plans should include the nuclear deterrent" (Brahma, 1993, p. 122). On January 1972, Bhutto held a secret meeting of the country's top scientists and engineers at Multan, where he committed his government to acquiring nuclear power and equipment (Spector, 1990, pp. 89-91). Bhutto attempted to purchase a reprocessing facility that would have enable it to extract weapons-grade plutonium from spent nuclear fuel from France. Washington pressurised Paris and Islamabad into cancelling the deal, after which Pakistan clandestinely acquired the technology to enrich uranium. In Pakistan, nuclear technology became linked to power, status and national security after an Indian nuclear test explosion in 1974. Bhutto, writing from his death cell in 1977, expressed this view: "We know that Israel and South Africa have full nuclear capability. The Christian, Jewish and Hindu civilisations have this capability. The communist powers also possess it. Only the Islamic civilisation is without it, but that position is about to change" (Bhutto, 1979, pp. 18-45).

After learning from intelligence reports that Pakistan is acquiring ability to make nuclear weapons, Carter Administration stopped all aids to Pakistan. This was done in accordance with amendment of '76 Nuclear Proliferation Act' which prohibited economic and military assistance to any country that obtained equipment for nuclear enrichment without placing it under internal safeguards (New York Times, April 7, 1979). Pakistan denied its plans to develop nuclear weapons and denounced the US decision to terminate American aid and suspicion that such nuclear programme was under way. It further attributed that the US policy was under the Zionist circles (New York Times, April 9, 1979).

It was held that the Carter Administration cut off the economic aid to Pakistan for building their nuclear weapons plant, but no such action was taken against India by last three Administrations for exploding the plutonium device; it was also known that eighty two years old Indian Prime Minister Desai promised not to authorise second atomic test but his successors may not have felt that they were bound by any such promises (New York Times, April 16, 1979).

Carter Administration's plans to sell Pakistan up to 50 Northrop F-5E Tiger fighter planes, to give help on nuclear power to Pakistan, agreement to restrict production of nuclear weapons, offer of diplomatic backing for controversial Pakistanis proposal and calling for free nuclear zone in South Asia, reflected the Administration's growing concern over possibility of nuclear arms race between Pakistan and India. Some top officials circles believe that Administration would have lost some leverage on Pakistan's nuclear plans by halting over $80 million in economic assistance (New York Times, April 17, 1979). India rejected the Parliament's demand to manufacture atomic bomb, because of reports that Pakistan was attempting to achieve nuclear-weapons capability (New York Times, April 21, 1979). Carter Administration's advisers said that Calif Company sold Pakistani components which would have been used in producing weapons-grade uranium (New York Times, May 2, 1979). India reviewed its defence policy in the light of reports that Pakistan had plans on developing nuclear explosion capability (New York Times, May 4, 1979).

The Carter Administration upheld the avoidance of the atomic arms-race between India and Pakistan, and promoted the idea of nuclear-free zone. The proposal was to be backed by security guarantees from US, USSR and China. India and Pakistan were called to reject acquisition of nuclear weapons and accept internal safeguard measures on existing nuclear facility; at the same time, the administration required that the guarantor countries should commit not to threaten nations with nuclear attacks (New York Times, May 27, 1979). Indian Prime Minister Charan Singh reportedly kept the nation's nuclear will open; this issue had become a matter of increasing concern and reports claimed that Pakistan was developing nuclear weapons (New York Times, July 28, 1979).

Officials from Pakistan were perplexed by, as what they regarded, US's short sighted punitive policies on the issue of nuclear arms development; they held that the stand taken by US was foolish. Western diplomats attributed Pakistan's mild and almost deferential attitude towards this issue as the reason of being rebuffed by US and the country realised that it needed American support at this juncture of looming possibilities of being singled out. (New York Times, August 9, 1979). Carter Administration and State department officials were weighing series of inducement including new offers of advanced conventional arms, imposition of economic sanctions and covert operations against uranium enrichment facility (New York Times, August 12, 1979).

Pakistan questioned US ambassador Arthur W Hummel Junior about his report in New York Times that claimed that American officials were considering covert action to prevent Pakistan from developing nuclear weapons; his report quoted that the State Department officials said that Pakistan was on the limit of developing an atomic bomb and had spurned several pleas not to do so, the report also mentioned that Administration officials were considering such options as offers of sophisticated but conventional military aid to Pakistan and other economic sanctions (New York Times, August 15, 1979). US State Department spokesman Thomas Reston, in response to the report, said that overall policy towards Pakistan was under constant review and rejected allegations of covert action. (*ibid*). Indian Prime Minister Charan Singh warned that India might be forced to develop nuclear weapons if Pakistan proceeded with its plans to assemble on atomic bomb. (New York Times, August 16, 1979).

Carter Administration's adviser said that they had received unconfirmed reports that Pakistan was preparing an underground test site for detonating a nuclear device, leading some of them to speculate that Pakistan might be much closer to building a nuclear bomb than previously suspected, Indian Prime Minister Charan Singh warned that India might be forced to reconsider its non-nuclear stance if Pakistan would go ahead with efforts to build a bomb. (New York Times, August 15, 1979).

US officials expected this India-Pakistan armed race despite efforts by US and other countries to prevent such a competition; several officials said that the US policy during last decade may have actually spurred the race; threat of nuclear race between India and Pakistan were viewed as a particularly disturbing prospect which had become a cause of deep political and religious enmity between the two powers (New York Times, August 24, 1979).

US State Secretary, Vance and Pakistani Acting Foreign Minister Agha Shahi discussed on October 17 without resolving serious differences about Pakistani nuclear programme (New York Times, October 19, 1979).

Pakistan continued to seek nuclear arms capacity despite US warnings, US Senate Department officials said that this could undercut Washington's plan to provide it with military support (New York Times, February 28, 1980). President Zia-ul-Haq said Pakistan determined to continue its nuclear programme for peaceful purpose because it was vital for country's economy (New York Times, March 11, 1980). US Secretary of State, Alexander M Haig Junior favoured modification of legislation policy bars of aid to Pakistan because of its secret programme to develop nuclear devices, Congressional committee hearing portrait said that Reagan Administration sought to avoid isolating such countries as Pakistan so that they were not drivon 'towards nuclear option' (New York Times, March 19, 1981).

Representative Jonathan B Bingham opposed Haig's idea for change in Nuclear Non-Proliferation Act and contended that such action would send Pakistan signal that it could develop nuclear weapons without risking its security relationship with US (New York Times, March 19, 1981).

Long standing dispute over nuclear issue between US and Pakistan should pose no barriers to improved relations between two nations and to increased economic and military aid. (New York Times, April 3, 1981). Under Secretary James L Buckley said Pakistan had assured to Reagan Administration that it was neither developing nor planning to develop nuclear weapons. (New York Times, June 25, 1981). Buckley said nuclear detonation could cost Pakistanis $3.2 billion aid package, as per testimony of house of Foreign Affairs comment, President Zia had assured Buckley that Pakistan would not develop nuclear weapons but refused to rule out the possibility to explode peaceful nuclear device (New York Times, September 7, 1981). US Senate votes for the renewal of military and economic aid to Pakistan (New York Times, October 21, 1981). Out of 51 votes of US Senate 46 votes were required to cut off foreign aid if Pakistan detonated nuclear device (New York Times, October 22, 1981). Unidentified Indian official achieved Senate decision for equating Indian and Pakistani nuclear programmes. (New York Times, October 23, 1981). US Senate in course of debate on foreign aid bill, votes to allow resumption of economic and military aid to Pakistan, if Presidential report certified that Pakistan was not developing nuclear weapons (*ibid*). Editorial supports Senate's action in lifting of ban on aid to Pakistan, particularly with added stipulation that Pakistan would forfeit aid if it explodes nuclear device (New York Times, November 2, 1981). US Under Secretary of State James L Buckley defends Reagan Administration's decision to sell 40 F-16 fighter planes to Pakistan (New York Times, November 3, 1981). House of Representative Foreign Affairs Committee rejected resolution on opposing sale of 40 F-16 planes to Pakistan. (New York Times, November 20, 1981)

House of Representative and Senate conferces reached compromise on aid bill, permitted the President to waive for 30 days the assurance he was required to give as condition for continuance of aid to Pakistan, the assurance being that Pakistan was not involved in transfer or receipt of nuclear device, or detonation of such device; Congress was required to act after 30 days waiver was up (New York Times, December 15, 1981).

US intelligence reported that Pakistan would be able to detonate nuclear device within next three years, but it was not likely to do so because of fear of jeopardizing Reagan

Administration's $3.2 billion military and economic aid programme (New York Times, January 26, 1982). Pakistan begins soliciting bids for purchase of new nuclear reactor from West, this was described by American officials as likely to complicate American efforts to block sale of nuclear arms technology to Pakistan (New York Times, December 5, 1982). Zia spoke at Foreign Policy Association luncheon, that Pakistan had neither desire nor means for making nuclear device; he said US aid package for Pakistan had laid foundation for 'enduring relationship'; says his government was determined to pursue relationship of 'neighbourly operation' with India (New York Times, December 10, 1982). United States mission to India and Pakistan was praised in Pakistan but criticised in India for the suggestion that the two nations undertake 'regional initiative' to avert nuclear arms race in the subcontinent; US officials said next steps in reducing tension could come at a possible meeting (New York Times, September 22, 1985).

Indian Prime Minister Rajiv Gandhi invited Pakistan's President Zia-ul-Haq to attend inauguration of nuclear power plant in India, which he attended next month, so that he could see for himself that Indian nuclear power programme did not pose any threat to his country (New York Times, December 1, 1985). Pakistani Prime Minister Mohammad Khan Junejo arrived in Washington on a three-day visit (New York Times, July 16, 1986). Pakistani Prime Minister, assured the Reagan Administration that Pakistan was not developing nuclear bomb; the statement followed US warning that such development would result in the termination of US financial assistance (New York Times, July 17, 1986). State Department concluded that Pakistan was probably involved in a plot to smuggle material for nuclear weapons out of United States, and reportedly recommended President Reagan to enforce law that would require cut off in aid to Pakistan (New York Times, January 14, 1988).

Pakistani General Mirza Aslam Beg reported successful testing of two types of surface-tosurface missiles; he also said that Pakistan might produce its own tanks within two years (New

York Times, February 6, 1988). Bhutto's government was removed from power because the United States disapproved of Bhutto's nuclear ambitions. He was a dynamic and outstanding politician who became a victim of opposition. He defied a superpower and in the process sacrificed his government and ultimately his life for the sake of national interest and survival. Thus, the Pakistani nuclear weapons programme took shape in 1976 when Dr. Abdul Qadeer Khan, a German-trained metallurgist, returned to Pakistan from the Netherlands and ultimately an enrichment facility at Kahuta based on the stolen blueprints from Almelo gas centrifuge enrichment plant was completed in 1985. Pakistan also has a small pilot plant at Sihala, the existence of which was acknowledged by Zia-ul-Haq. However, the Kahuta enrichment facility began to produce weapons-grade uranium in the Mid-1980s and this plant produces uranium enriched to more than the relatively innocuous five per cent level. (*New York Times* (Magazine), March 6, 1988, p. 38) Thus, it is the uranium enrichment programme that provided the decisive breakthrough for Pakistan in the area of weapongrade material production. The 1980s saw Pakistan's achievement of the target of designing a nuclear weapon and the acquisition of important hardware. Dr. Abdul Qadeer Khan, the mastermind behind the establishment of the Kahuta enriching plant, was able to announce his country's success in breaking the Western monopoly and exceeding the five per cent level in uranium enrichment (The New York Times, March 6, 1988).

Pakistan's crossing of the five per cent "red line" was not challenged by the United States because Pakistan was at that time a key ally, providing the crucial link in the CIA's effort to smuggle billions of dollars of weapons to Afghan guerrillas attempting to drive out the Soviet Union from Afghanistan. (Smith, *New York Times* (Magazine), March 6, 1988) The Reagan administration was keen to supply Pakistan with sophisticated air-to-air missiles, and key congressional committees also approved $3.2 billion for five years (1981-1985) as aid package to Pakistan. (Omang, *Washington Post,* 21 March 1985) In March 1986, the Reagan administration announced that it would provide Pakistan a second six-year (1985-1991) aid package worth of $4.2 billion. From this point onward, the Reagan administration was aware that Pakistan had achieved capability to build nuclear arms or assemble the components (Boyd, New York Times, 17 July 1986). According to Milt Bearden (a senior CIA officer in Pakistan from 1986 - 1989), in the early 1986 the Soviets and Indians talked Pakistan's nuclear issue with the US diplomats in an effort to isolate Pakistan from the Afghan issue but the US officials refused to discuss this matter and helped to create the conditions to produce weapons grade material (New York Times, 30 May 1998). According to the Tass report, the Reagan administration allowed Pakistan to increase their self-defence ability and Pakistan's nuclear capability was significantly improved during the years of 1985-86 in order to prevent the Soviets moving towards the Persian Gulf. During those years, Pakistan set up a worldwide smuggling ring to buy, copy or steal nuclear weapons technology. Some sources claimed that during this time, Pakistan conducted two nuclear tests and rapidly assembled at least one nuclear device in the event of a future war (Spector, 1990, pp. 95). The Zia regime was completely successful in its clandestine efforts to secure classified designs of a centrifuge-based uranium enrichment plant and in obtaining a number of critical sub-systems, components and materials. Zia strongly supported Pakistan's nuclear programme and refused to accept full-scope safeguards. He said: "We shall eat crumbs but will not allow our national interest to be compromised in any manner what-so-ever". Zia admitted, "Pakistan can build a (nuclear) bomb whenever it wishes. Once you have acquired the technology, which Pakistan has, you can do whatever you like" (Doerner, Time, 30 March 1987, p. 42).

He deliberately took calculated risks, and skilfully exploited the international environment in the wake of the Afghan crisis. Although there was a lack of hard information concerning Pakistan's nuclear status, it was assumed that the country had the ability to manufacture atomic weapons and had become a de facto nuclear weapon state. An understanding of the historical and recent sources of Pakistan's perception of the US was critical to understanding why, to Pakistan, US nuclear policy was simply more evident of its duplicity and untrustworthiness. This section describes Pakistan's perception of the US, historically, and in relation to current events. In ways that are similar to Iran, Pakistan's historic narrative is replete with "a sense of wrong doing and injustices, betrayals of trust and treaties, abandonment by allies, and victimisation due to religion, race and colour" (Khan, *Strategic Insights*, Vol. 4, No., October10, 2005, p. 2).

The relationship fell apart during the 1970s, as new strains arose over Pakistan's efforts to respond to India's 1974 nuclear test by seeking its own nuclear capability. With the 1980 Soviet invasion of Afghanistan, however, US priorities shifted again, and Pakistan was again viewed as a frontline ally in the effort to block Soviet expansionism. In 1981, the Reagan Administration offered Islamabad a five-year, $3.2 billion aid package, and turned a blind eye to Pakistan's nuclear programme - even waiving specific sanctions mandated by law (Alan Kronstadt, *CRS Issue Brief for Congress*, March 6, 2006, p. 3). The certification requirement is the most recent in a series of linked non-proliferation sections of the Foreign Assistance Act (FAA) that have attempted to use the threat of an aid cut off as an incentive to Pakistan to discontinue its efforts to acquire a nuclear weapons capability. The most pertinent provisions are noted below.

The basic non-proliferation provision affecting Pakistan is Section 101 of the Arms Export Control Act (an expanded version of what was formerly Section 669 of the FAA). This provision forbids aid to countries that acquire nuclear enrichment facilities that are not under the inspection and safeguards system of the International Atomic Energy Agency (IAEA). The Carter Administration, in April 1979, invoked Section 669 and suspended aid to Pakistan after intelligence information confirmed that Pakistan was building a secret uranium enrichment facility.

Section 620E of the FAA, adopted by Congress in 1981 following the December 1979 Soviet invasion of Afghanistan, sought to reconcile US nuclear non-proliferation policy with urgent US regional security interests. Unlike Section 669, Section 620E is Pakistan-specific, having been adopted to reaffirm a 1959 US-Pakistan bilateral security agreement and to permit the resumption of US military and economic assistance to Pakistan by granting authority to the President to waive Section 669 in Pakistan's case if he decides that to do so is in the national interest. The waiver authority was granted initially for a period of six years, facilitating the Reagan Administration's commitment of a six-year, $3.2 billion package of economic and military aid to Pakistan. The waiver authority was periodically extended by Congress after that date but was subjected to increasing conditions, especially the Section 620E (e) certification requirement.

In 1985, in the face of growing congressional impatience with Pakistan's evident determination to continue development of its nuclear option, Congress added subsection (e) to existing Section 620E, placing a new limitation on the President's ability to grant waivers to application of the then Section 669. Subsection 669 (e), the Pressler Amendment states: "no assistance shall be furnished to Pakistan and no military equipment or technology shall be sold or transferred to Pakistan pursuant to the authorities contained in this Act or any other Act" unless the President makes an annual certification to Congress that Pakistan does not possess a nuclear explosive device and that the proposed aid will reduce significantly the risk that it will possess one.

Larry Lee Pressler (born on March 29, 1942) is a US Republican politician. He was the first Vietnam veteran to be elected to the United States Senate. Pressler was also the key sponsor of the Pressler Amendment which prohibited Pakistan from developing a nuclear weapon. The US Congress passed the "Pressler Amendment," in 1985 and it required the President to certify that Pakistan had not had nuclear weapons every year. This amendment was championed by Senator Larry

Pressler (R-SD), in this amendment, if the President does not issue such certification, Pakistan cannot not get any foreign aid from the US.-Pakistan pursuant to the authorities contained in this Act or any other Act unless the President makes an annual certification to Congress that Pakistan does not possess a nuclear explosive device and that the proposed aid will reduce significantly the risk that it will possess one" (http://www.fas.org/spp/starwars/crs/90-149.htm).

On March 28, 1984, the Congress Committee adopted an amendment offered by Sen. Cranston and myself Senator John Glenn. Providing that no assistance shall be furnished and no military equipment or technology shall be sold or transferred to Pakistan unless the President could first certify that Pakistan does not possess a nuclear explosive device, is not developing a nuclear device, and is not acquiring goods to make such a device. On April 3, 1984, the Committee narrowly voted to reconsider. This amendment and adopted instead a substitute offered by Senator Pressler, Mathias and Percy, which tied the continuation of aid and military sales to two certification conditions: 1st that Pakistan does not possess a nuclear explosive device; and 2nd one that new aid will reduce significantly the risk that Pakistan will possess such a device. This was enacted on another bill in August 1985, has come to be called the 'Pressler' amendment. In this amendment made binding what had been an official policy, namely that aid would reduce the risk of nuclear proliferation. It also clarified-by its broad prohibition on all arms transfers under any US law-that a failure to meet these standards would lead to a cut off of not only assistance but of military sales as well. According to presser Pakistan's advances towards the bomb, new rationalisations kept flowing out from Foggy Bottom for continuing transfers of arms and aid for of non-proliferation issues brings that how the Pressler amendment and other relevant laws were implemented. Pressler has long believed that continued arms exports to Pakistan was no way to halt its bomb programme, but when one considers that of the 50 nuclear weapon-related events that have been cited in the submission to the Committee, three-quarters of them occurred after the Pressler amendment was enacted, it becomes glaringly apparent that the Reagan and Bush administrations willfully violated not only the Pressler amendment but several other nuclear non-proliferation laws as well. (http://fas.org/news/pakistan/1992/920731.htm)

In 1985, in the face of growing congressional impatience with Pakistan's evident determination to continue development of its nuclear option, Congress added subsection (e) to existing Section 620E, placing a new limitation on the President's ability to grant waivers to application of the then Section 669. Subsection (e), the Pressler Amendment: states "no assistance shall be furnished to Pakistan and no military equipment or technology shall be sold or transferred to Pakistan pursuant to the authorities contained in this Act or any other Act" unless the President makes an annual certification to Congress that Pakistan does not possess a nuclear explosive device and that the proposed aid will reduce significantly the risk that it will possess one. This section was the focus of action in the 104th Congress. The addition by Congress in 1985 of subsection (e) to Section 620E in 1985 responded to clear evidence that despite US admonitions, Pakistan was continuing to employ various covert means to work towards achieving a nuclear weapons capability. During the mid-1980s it became increasingly clear that the US support of Pakistan's conventional defense requirements was not working to limit its nuclear ambitions, as had been hoped. Eventually, US intelligence agencies acquired evidence that indicated strongly that Pakistan had crossed the nuclear threshold in some manner. (http://www.nuclearinternet\ 90149 Pakistan Aid Cutoff US Non proliferation and Foreign. htm) Aside from Afghanistan, the most problematic element in Pakistan's security policy was the nuclear question. President Zia had inherited a pledge that for domestic reasons, he could not discard but continued the nuclear development programme. Zia inherited an ambitious programme from Bhutto and continued to develop it out of the realisation that, despite Pakistan's newly acquired weaponry, it could never match India's conventional power and that India either had, or shortly could develop, its own nuclear weapons.

In 1985, the Solarz Amendment was added to prohibit aid to countries that attempt to import nuclear commodities from the United States. In the same year, the Pressler Amendment was passed, referring specifically to Pakistan. It said that if that nation possessed a nuclear device, aid would be suspended. Many of these amendments could be waived if the president declared that it was in the national interests of the United States to continue assistance. Even after the invasion of Afghanistan, Pakistan almost exhausted United State's tolerance, including bungled attempts to illegally acquire United States nuclear-relevant technology and a virtual public admission in 1987 by the head of Pakistan's nuclear programme that the country had developed a weapon. As long as Pakistan remained vital to the United State's interested in Afghanistan, however, no action was taken to cut off United States support. For the remainder of Zia's tenure, the United States generally ignored Pakistan's endeavours of developing a nuclear programme. But Zia's death was followed by another cut off of aid which was caused Pakistan's persistent drive towards nuclear development.

Initially, Pakistani govt. to handle the bilateral nuclear relationship with India led nowhere, but a significant step was a non-formalised 1985 agreement that neither India nor Pakistan would attack the other's nuclear facilities. Zia asked India to agree to several steps to end the potential nuclear arms race in the subcontinent. One of these measures was the simultaneous signing of the Treaty on the Non-Proliferation of Nuclear Weapons. The second step was a joint agreement for inspection of all nuclear sites by the International Atomic Energy Agency. Pakistan also proposed a pact between the two countries to allow for mutual inspection of sites. And, finally, Pakistan proposed a South Asian nuclear-free zone. It appeared that Zia was looking for a way to terminate the costly Pakistani programme. But in order to sell this idea in Pakistan, he required some concessions from India. Termination would also get him out of difficulties the programme was causing with the United States, including the curtailment of aid in 1979. (http://www. nuclear internet\Pakistan Nuclear Weapons.htm)

Congressional Attitude

Congress has very limited ability to promote either a resolution on the Kashmir issue or a regional non-proliferation accord, although it has already made the latter an official objective of US policy. Nor is Congress in a strong position to obtain greater adherence to US non-proliferation policy goals on the part of other bilateral aid donors or multilateral institutions. An active US effort to broker a regional accord or promote a resolution of the Kashmir issue would likely require Congress to provide flexibility to the Administration regarding the Pressler Amendment, since the removal of sanctions would likely be an important incentive to Pakistan.

The President signed and sent to Congress waivers to the law that would require a cut off in aid to Pakistan under the Symington and the Solarz Amendments because of activities in the nuclear weapons development area. This waiver action was based on the recognition that disrupting one of the pillars of the US relationship with Pakistan would be counterproductive for the strategic interests of the United States, destabilising for South Asia, and unlikely to achieve the non-proliferation objectives. Pakistan Government aware and concern of their nuclear programme. Despite these problem areas, there are certain crucial nonproliferation criteria which Pakistan continues to honour. The United States insisted on the maintenance of these restraints even as we work with Pakistan on the progress in the areas of concern. A very important event in this quarter was the restoration of American aid to Pakistan in December 1987. The US Congress finally approved a follow on $4.02 billion aid package to Pakistan with a two year waiver of a key nuclear non-proliferation law. (Tahir, Ahmed Naved).

It is important to recall that the American Congress had voted a 105-day suspension of aid in August 1987 on suspicion that the Pakistan government was involved in the attempted import of some strategic nuclear material from the US by Arshad Pervez, a Canadian of Pakistani origin. Islamabad's atomic energy programme had become suspicious in the American eyes because of this incident. The approval of the aid package by the congress has cleared Pakistan of the Charges levelled against it of trying to obtain weapons grade nuclear technology. It certain Senate and House of Representatives proposals had been passed by the Congress, Pakistan would have had to open its nuclear facilities to international inspection. Since the discloser of the Arshad Pervez affair, the anti-Pakistan lobby in US Congres-sional circles had been demanding a permanent stoppage of aid to Pakistan unless Islamabad provided "credible assurance" that it was not producing weaponsgrade nuclear material since that meant international inspection of Pakistan's nuclear facilities, it was firmly rejected by Islamabad. (*ibid*)

A key Congressional panel, in early December approved a new proposal by which US aid to Pakistan would be restored without Islamabad having to open its nuclear facilities to international inspection and even if it produced weapons-grade material in competition with India. The Continuation of such military and Economic aid, however, would be subjected to presidential waivers with the administration pursuing a regional approach towards non-proliferation in the area. This approach was upheld by the powerful Senate Appropriations Committee as it unanimously adopted a detailed but complex legislation drafted by Senator Daniel Lnouye, a Democrat. In effect it was aimed at including both India and Pakistan to accept international safeguards in their nuclear facilities. (*ibid, pp. iii-iv*)

Congressional aids and administration officiates described the bill, which was to go to the Senate, as a "major victory" for Pakistan and its lobby in Capitol Hill. The bill accepted Pakistan's contention that there can be no meaningful non-proliferation in South Asia without taking into consideration India's extensive and advanced nuclear programme. The Indian lobby in the Congressional circles began, at this juncture, a concerted campaign to stop the passage of the bill in the form put forward by the congressional panel. The Indian ambassador in Washington, P.K. Paul told Under Secretary of State, Michael Armacost that his government was seriously concerned over the move to "equate" India's nuclear programme with that of Pakistan. (*ibid, p. iv*). When the US Ambassador to India, John Gunther Dean, called on the Indian Prime Minister Mr. Rajeev Gandhi, the latter expressed India's concern over the attempt of the US Senate subcommittee to equate India's nuclear programme with that of Pakistan. Mr. Gandhi's contention was that India's nuclear programme was for peaceful purpose whereas Pakistan's was weapon's oriented. Elaborating on this issue, an Indian Spokesman said that the recommendations of the subcommittees are based on the untenable premises of equating India's "open" and "peaceful" nuclear programme with Pakistan's "covert efforts" to acquire nuclear weapons capability. He stated *"we are opposed to both vertical* and horizontal proliferation of nuclear weapons. India has not accepted and does not intend to accept that the safeguard should be applied uniformly and without discrimination to all nuclear *activities in all countries"*. (*ibid, pp. vi-v*)

The final action came after long deliberation in Joint Conference Committee of the House of Representatives and the Senate. It represented a compromise between the positions taken by the two houses on the resumption of economic and military assistance to Pakistan. The US Congress on 17th December 1987 approved a follow on $4.02 billion aid package to Pakistan, which placed no fresh conditions but retained the 2 Yz year waiver of the key nuclear non-proliferation law. A Pakistan embassy spokesman described the measure as "reasonably good". He said it demonstrated the realisation on Capitol Hill Administration as well of the importance of Pakistan to the United States. (*ibid, pp. v-iv*). The Conference Committee, the ultimate Congressional body, allocated $220 million in economic assistance and $260 million in military assistance in 1988, the first year of the new aid package. The administration had recommended $250 million and $290 million for economic and military assistance; $30 million was to be on the grant basis. According to Congressional sources the funding levels for

Pakistan did not suffer the kind of drastic cuts that other friends of the United States, with the exception of Egypt and Israel, experienced in 1988-the year of serious budgetary constraints. The Pakistan Ambassador in the US declared "Pakistan has emerged with its principles intact" and it has "not been singled out on the nuclear issue." However, by dropping the Appropriation Committee's recommendation that a regional approach be adopted towards non-proliferation, the Senate has once again confirmed its Policy of adopting a bilateral approach on nuclear issue in its dealings with countries of South Asia. In this respect, Pakistan has always suffered through the discriminatory approach adopted by US. While it has been suggested on many occasions that Pakistan proves it nuclear innocence, other countries, who were also on the atomic threshold, such as Israel, South Africa, Brazil and even India enjoyed a greater degree of freedom in pursuing their nuclear programmes without the threat of a cut down of American technical or financial assistance. For instance, during Rajeev Gandhi's visit to the United States in October 1987, the Indian Prime Minister had reportedly invited some US aircraft manufacturers and defence contractors to make a proposal for transfer of technology about metal alloys used for military aircraft (the Indians hoped to manufacture light combat aircraft). If this was to come through, it would have been the second deal of a major military significance between the United States and India, the first on high technology computers having been finalised already. (*ibid, p. vi*)

Would the US, in return for the transfer of such technology, be able to prevail upon India so as to make it sign the NPT? Since the new aid package requires that American President should certify to Congress that Pakistan was not producing highly enriched uranium or separated plutonium, it would mean that Pakistan's nuclear programme can at any moment be made the pretext for suspension for aid. Besides, aid to Pakistan had been unequivocally linked with the Afghanistan issue. It was absolutely clear that Pakistan was receiving the aid specifically to enable it to continue supporting the Afghan resistance. Thus, with the last and probably conclusive round of Geneva talks quite close, American aid to Pakistan could be cut off because of a qualitative change in the geo-strategic environment of the region (Tahir, Pakistan Foreign Policy, January 1987, pp. iii-vii).

The President's action is preceded by months of extensive consultations with Congress. We have achieved an understanding on the general approach which is reflected in approval by Congress of a 30-month waiver of the Symington amendment and near- full funding for Pakistan for FY 1988. The Administration pledged to continue pressing Pakistan away from a nuclear weapons option and was obliged to certify annually that Pakistan does not possess nuclear weapons.

The reasons that convinced the Administration to waive the Symington amendment also applied to the Solarz amendment, where the waiver applied only retroactively. The Government of Pakistan pledged that procedures will be tightened so as to ensure an end to procurement activities in the United States and that the latter would continue to monitor Pakistan's procurement activities so as to ensure compliance with the new procedures.

There was no diminution in the President's commitment to restrain the spread of nuclear weapons in the Indian subcontinent or elsewhere. The US continued to urge Pakistan and India to discuss measures which might be taken to reduce the threat of a nuclear arms race in South Asia. As arms control negotiations between the United States and the Soviet Union begin to bear fruit and set an example, the Administration was to seek still further ways to make this commitment effective (http:// www. white house statement_ ai_6761457.htm)

Pentagon's Perception

This section examines the development in various fields of US-Pakistan relations during Ronald Reagan's period. It was due to the compulsion of the Afghan crisis that both countries came closer to each other. This period also saw the Nuclear Proliferation so this section focuses on these two important issues taking into account the attitude of Congress and

Pentagon's Perception. The 1976 Arms Export Control Act required Congress to receive notice of proposed arms sales exceeding $14 million that do not involve Australia, Japan, New Zealand, or NATO members, all of which had a higher reporting threshold and a shorter congressional review period. In all other cases, law-makers have 30 calendar days to block a notified deal by passing a joint resolution of disapproval.

The Pentagon detailed plans to provide Pakistan with 36 F-16C/D combat aircraft, an assortment of F-16 engines and upgrade kits, and thousands of bombs and missiles, including 500 advanced air-to-air missiles. Describing Pakistan as a "vital ally", the Pentagon stated the arms would be used in fighting terrorist outfits, such as Al Qaeda, and "would not significantly reduce India's quantitative or qualitative military advantage" in the region. With India, the Bush administration pursued closer military ties, including offering F-16s, as well as an enhanced civil nuclear trade relationship.

The United States and Pakistan have tangled for years over sales of F-16s, which can be built or modified to deliver nuclear weapons. The United States provided Pakistan with 40 F-16s during the 1980s. Still, the administration's formal announcement to deliver three dozen new F-16s to Pakistan sparked an uproar from House International Relations Committee members, who convened a July 20 hearing to upbraid a senior administration official about the deal. Although some committee members faulted aspects of the sale, much of the outcry stemmed from the administration's failure to follow traditional procedures. Specifically, the administration did not give the 20-day advance notice typical for formal arms sales notifications. This period is intended to allow reservations about a particular sale to be expressed and worked out privately to avoid public quarrels.

At the hearing, Committee Chairman Henry Hyde (R-Ill.) charged that neglecting the prenotification process constituted a "deliberate and, we believe, wholly inappropriate manoeuvre by the State Department to diminish the Congress' lawful oversight of arms sales". Consequently, he said, "long-standing congressional concerns about the potential for technology diversion remain". The Department of State administers arms sales policies and licensing, while the Pentagon helps negotiate and implement US government weapons transfers to foreign governments. Hyde and Lantos introduced legislation the same day that, among other things, would have codified the 20-day pre-notification practice that the legislation was no longer under consideration because the administration provided assurances that the Pakistani case "was not a precedent and would not happen again". Some legislators objected to the sale for reasons other than procedure. Republicans argued that F-16s were not the proper weapons for Pakistan because the planes are suited to fighting "sophisticated air forces, not the Taliban, not radical Islam", and could be converted to deliver nuclear weapons. Some expert responded that Pakistan had employed F-16s in "hundreds of missions in the global war on terror". He further said that the F-16s to be delivered to Pakistan "will not be nuclear capable" and that Islamabad has "given no indications that they want to modify F-16s to deliver nuclear weapons". The Arms Export Control Act prohibits any US arms recipient from using imported weapons "for purposes other than those for which furnished".

Whether Pakistan configured previously imported US F-16s for nuclear missions is uncertain. Political-military affairs bureau spokesperson Jason Greer declined to answer Arms Control Today's questions on the subject. A July according to a by the Congressional Research Service (CRS), which conducts studies for law-makers, noted that "the 32 F-16s that Pakistan already fields are believed to be nuclear capable". Democratic Republition Gary Ackerman (N.Y.) and Edward Markey (Mass.) proposed separate legislations to block the sale, but neither effort garnered much support. Markey's bill sought to tie the F-16 sales to Pakistan halting construction of a new heavy-water reactor, which was exposed publicly in July by the Washingtonbased non-governmental Institute for Science and International Security. Administration officials, who claimed Washington knew of the project for "some time", said they are urging Pakistan not to use the reactor for military purposes, but Markey argued on the House floor July 26 that US-supplied F-16s might someday be carrying nuclear bombs made possible by this uncompleted facility. http://www.armscontrol.org/act/2006-09/armsbuys.asp

In 1980s Barlow's intelligence work began at the CIA, where he analysed nuclear programmes in other countries. He contributed to the National Intelligence estimates and presented findings to national security agencies, the White House and congressional committees. He received the CIA's Exceptional Accomplishment Award in 1988. The next year, he became the first intelligence officer for the Office of the Secretary of Defence, charged with analysing nuclear weapons developments involving foreign governments. He answered to Gerald Brubaker, the acting director of the Office of Non-Proliferation. Supervisor of Brubaker was Victor Rostow, the principal director. Rostow reported to Deputy Assistant Secretary James Hinds, who reported to Assistant Secretary Stephen Hadley. Washington Post (July, 7, 2007), www.informationlibration.com/id=22864).

At the time, the government was poised to sell $1.4 billion worth of new F-16 fighter planes to Pakistan to help the Mujaheddin fight the Soviets in Afghanistan. But Congress, through two laws passed in 1985, had forbidden the sale of any equipment that could be used to deliver nuclear bombs. Barlow wrote an analysis for then-Secretary Dick Cheney that concluded the planned F-16 sale violated this law. Drawing on detailed, classified studies, Barlow wrote about Pakistan's ability, intentions and activities to deliver nuclear bombs using F-16s it had acquired before the law was passed. Barlow discovered later that someone rewrote his analysis so that it endorsed the sale of the F-16s. Arthur Hughes, the deputy assistant secretary of defence, testified to Congress that using the F-16s to deliver nuclear weapons "far exceeded the state of art in Pakistan" something Barlow knew to be untrue. (*ibid*)

In 1989, Barlow told Brubaker, Rostow and Michael MacMurray, the Pakistan desk officer in charge of military sales to Pakistan who prepared Hughes's testimony, that Congress had been misled. "They clearly didn't want the non-proliferation policy to get in the way of their regional policy", Gallucci said. "They were worried someone like Rich (Barlow), in his stickler approach, would insist that if there's going to be testimony on the Hill about the F-16 aircraft, that the answers be full and truthful. He was a thorn in their side, and they went after him. And they did a very good job of screwing up his life". "There have been times on that issue when I specifically sensed that people thought we could somehow construct a policy on a house of cards that the Congress wouldn't know what the Pakistanis were doing", Wolfowitz told the Senate Armed Services Committee. (*ibid*)

That left him without the $89,500 annual pension and health insurance that Barlow believes the government owes him. He faces no organised opposition now but has so far been stymied by government's inertia, the passage of time, congressional procedural errors, and endless debates over how much money he's due and the proper legislative vehicle for his pension. Twenty Senators and eight legislative committees have considered his case over the years without resolving it, suggesting a larger dilemma: No process exists to compensate fired whistle-blowers in the intelligence field, and those who retaliate against them face no criminal penalties. (http://www.informationliberation.com/?id=22864) (*ibid*)

References

Bhutto, Z. A.(1979), "*If I am Assassinated*," New Delhi: Vikas.

Boyd, Gerald M (1986), 'Pakistan Denies Developing Bomb', *New York Times*, July 17, 1986.

Buzan, Barry, "Peace, Power, and Security: Contending Concepts in the Study of International Relations" [Online :Web], URL:http://jpr.sagepub.com/cgi/content/refs/21/2/109

Chellaney, Brahma (1993), 'The Challenge of Nuclear Arms Control in South Asia', *Survival*, Vol. 35, No.3, autumn 1993.

Doerner, William R. (1987), 'Knocking at the Nuclear Door,' *Time*, March 30, 1987.

Frankel, Francine R.(1986), "Play the India Card," *Foreign Policy* (Spring), 1986.

Gerald, M. Boyd, 'Pakistan Denies Developing Bomb', New York Times, 17 July 1986.

Handel, Michael (1981), *Weak States in the International System*, London: Frank Cass.

Handel, Michael, Weak States in the International System, 1981, p. 77.

Haqqani, Husain (2005), *Pakistan: Between Mosque and Military,* Washington, DC: Carnegie Endowment for International Peace.

Hedrick, Smith, 'A Bomb Ticks in Pakistan', New York Times (Magazine) 6 March 1988.

Hoyt, Timothy D., 2005, "*The Human Bone Manua"* USA:Elsevier.

Hoyt, Timothy D. and Lowell Dittmer (ed.) (2005), "Strategic Myopia: Pakistan's Nuclear Doctrine and Crisis Stability in South Asia," and in *South Asia's Nuclear Security Dilemma: India, Pakistan and China*, NY: ME Sharpe.

http:// www. white house statement_ ai_6761457.htm

http:// www. white house statement_ ai_6761457.htm

http://en.wikipedia.org/wiki/Foreign_relations_of_Afghanistan

http://en.wikipedia.org/wiki/Foreign_relations_of_Afghanistan

http://en.wikipedia.org/wiki/Foreign_relations_of_Afghanistan

http://en.wikipedia.org/wiki/Foreign_relations_of_Afghanistan

http://en.wikipedia.org/wiki/US-Afghanistan_relations

http://en.wikipedia.org/wiki/US-Afghanistan_relations

http://nuclear internet\U_S_-Pakistani nuclear Relations.htm

http://www. nuclear internet\Pakistan Nuclear Weapons.htm

http://www.armscontrol.org/act/2006_09/armsbuys.asp

http://www.armscontrol.org/act/2006_09/armsbuys.asp.

http://www.country-data.com/cgi-bin/query/r-9902.html

http://www.country-data.com/cgi-bin/query/r-9902.html

(New York Times, December 23, 1979)

(New York Times, January 3, 1980)

(New York Times, January 5, 1980)

(New York Times, January 10, 1980)

(New York Times, January 11, 1980)

(New York Times, January 13, 1980)

(New York Times, January 14, 1980)

(New York Times, January 15, 1980)

(New York Times, January 16, 1980)

(New York Times, January 17, 1980)

(New York Times, January 20, 1980)
(New York Times, January 21, 1980)
(New York Times, January 21, 1980)
(New York Times, January 23, 1980)
(New York Times, January 24, 1980)
(New York Times, January 27, 1980)
(New York Times, February 10, 1980)
(New York Times, February 15, 1980)
(New York Times, March 2, 1980)
(New York Times, March 7, 1980)
(New York Times, January 7, 1981)
(New York Times, January 9, 1981)
(New York Times, January15, 1981)
(New York Times, February 6, 1981)
(New York Times, March 8, 53. 1981)
(New York Times, May 18, 1984)
(New York Times, March 24, 1986)
(New York Times, October 16, 1986)
New York Times, October 17, 1986)
New York Times, October 23, 1986)
(New York Times, June 12, 1989)
(New York Times, June 19, 1988).
http://www.informationliberation.com/?id=22864
http://www.informationliberation.com/?id=22864
http://www.nuclear internet\90149 Pakistan Aid Cutoff U_S_ Nonproliferation and Foreign .htm
http://www.Nuclear internet\90149 Pakistan Aid Cutoff U_S_ Nonproliferation and Foreign.htm.
http://www.nuclear Internet\Pakistan Nuclear Weapons.htm
http://www.Nuclear internet\U_S_-Pakistani nuclear Relations.htm.
Joanne Omang, 'Report About Foreign Aid', Washington Post, 21 March 1985.
Kaiser, Karl (1989), "Non-proliferation and Nuclear Deterrence," *Survival*, Vol. 31, No. 2, March/April 1989.
Kaiser, Karl (1989), 'Non-Proliferation and Nuclear Deterrence', *Survival*, Vol. 31, No. 2, March/April 1989.
Kapur, Ashok (1987), *Pakistan's Nuclear Development*, London: Croom Helm.

Khan, Feroz Hassan (2005), "Comparative Strategic Culture: The Case of Pakistan," *Strategic Insights*, Vol. 4, No., October10, 2005.

Khan, Feroz Hassan (2005), *Strategic Insights*, Vol. 4, No. 10, October 2005.

Kronstadt, Alan (2006), "Pakistan-US Relations," *CRS Issue Brief for Congress*, IB94041 March 6, 2006.

Kronstadt, Alan (2006), *CRS Issue Brief for Congress*, March 6, 2006.

Kux, Dennis (2001), *The United States and Pakistan, 1947-2000: Disenchanted Allies,* Washington, DC: Woodrow Wilson Center Press.

Leonard S. Spector, Nuclear Ambitions: The Spread of Nuclear Weapons, Boulder: Westview Press, 1990, p. 95.

Leventhal, Paul L.(1992), 'Plugging the Leaks in Nuclear Export Control: Why Bother?', *ORBIS*, spring 1992.

Morgenthau, Hans 1964, 'The Four Paradoxes of Nuclear Strategy', *American Political Science Review*, Vol. 58, No. 1, March 1964.

Morgenthau, Hans J. (1964), "Balancing Proposition", *American Political Science Review*, Vol. 58, No. 1, March 1964.

Mukerjee Delip (1986), "India and the Soviet Union," *Washington Quarterly*, Spring,1986.

Naveed, Ahmad Tahir (January, 1988) Pakistan, Foreign Policy: A Quarterly Survey, Pakistan Horizon, Vol. 41, No. 1, Pakistan Institute of International Attairs.

New York Times, 30 May 1998.

New York Times, 6 March 1988.

O'Ballance, Edgar (1986), "Pakistan: On the Front Porch of Conflict," *Military Review*, March, 1986.

Omang, Joanne (1985), "Secret Votes Give Afghans $300 Million," *Washington Post*, October 10, 1985.

(New York Times, April 7, 1979)

(New York Times, April 9, 1979)

(New York Times, April 16, 1979)

(New York Times, April 17, 1979)

(New York Times, April 21, 1979)

(New York Times, May 2, 1979)

(New York Times, May 4, 1979)

(New York Times, May 27, 1979)

New York Times, July 28, 1979)

(New York Times, August 9, 1979)

(New York Times, August 12, 1979)
New York Times, August 15, 1979)
(New York Times, August 16, 1979)
(New York Times, August 15, 1979)
(New York Times, August 24, 1979)
(New York Times, October 19, 1979)
(New York Times, February 28, 1980)
New York Times, March 11, 1980)
(New York Times, March 19, 1981)
(New York Times, March 19, 1981)
(New York Times, April 3, 1981)
(New York Times, June 25, 1981)
(New York Times, September 7, 1981)
(Times, October 21, 1981)
(New York Times, October 22, 1981)
(New York Times, October 23, 1981)
(New York Times, November 2, 1981)
(New York Times, November 3, 1981)
(New York Times, November 20, 1981)
(New York Times, December 15, 1981)
(New York Times, January 26, 1982)
(New York Times, December 5, 1982)
(New York Times, December 10, 1982)
(New York Times, September 22, 1985)
(New York Times, December 1, 1985)
(New York Times, July 16, 1986)
(New York Times, July 17, 1986)
(New York Times, January 14, 1988)

Omang, Joanne (1985), 'Report About Foreign Aid', *Washington Post*, March 21,1985.

Paul L. Leventhal (1992), 'Plugging the Leaks in Nuclear Export Control: Why Bother?' *ORBIS*, spring 1992.

Pfaff, William (1998), 'Fear Religious Nationalism, Nuclear or Not', International Herald Tribune, June 3, 1998.

Rupert, James (1986), "Arms for Rebels Siphoned Off," *Washington Post*, January 16, 1986.

Smith, Hedrick (1988), 'A Bomb Ticks in Pakistan', *New York Times (Magazine)*, March 6, 1988.

Sorensen, George (1996), 'Individual Security and National Security', *Security Dialogue*, Vol. XXVII, No. 4, December4, 1996.

Sorensen, George (1996), 'Individual Security and National Security', *Security Dialogue*, Vol. XXVII, No. 4, December, 1996.

Spector, Leonard S (1990), *Nuclear Ambitions: The Spread of Nuclear Weapons*, Boulder: Westview Press.

Tahir, Naved Ahmad (1987), US Aid to Pakistan, Pakistan Foreign Policy-A Quarterly Survey, 1987.

Tahir-Kheli, Shirin (1982), The United States and Pakistan: The Evolution of an Influence Relationship, New York: Praeger.

Thayer, Bradley A. (1995), '*Security Studies*, Vol. V, No. 1, autumn 1995.

Waltz, Kenneth N. (1979), *"The Theory of International Politics"* USA: Random House.109.

Waltz, Kenneth N. (1981), *"The Spread of Nuclear Weapons: More May Be Better"*, London: International Institute for Strategic Studies, 1981.

Waltz, Kenneth N. (1995), *'The Spread of Nuclear Weapons: More May Be Better"*, Adelphi Paper, No. 171, London: International Institute of.

Waltz, Kenneth (1979), The Theory of International Politics, New York:

Washington Quarterly (Spring-1986), pp. 109-122.

Watson, Russell and Donna Foote (1986), "Avenging Angel," *Newsweek*, July 7, 1986.

Weintraub, Richard (1986), "Pakistanis Deny Nuclear-Arms Report," *Washington Post*, November 5, 1986.

William R. Doerner, *Time*, 30 March 1987, p. 42.

Wolfers, Arnold (1962), 'National Security as an Ambiguous Symbol: Discord and Collaboration, Baltimore: John Hopkins University Press.

Chapter 3

Frontline State Dimensions and Consequences

This chapter focuses on the US strategy towards Pakistan during Afghan crisis. The chapter also analyses the cooperation between the two countries in military and economic assistance and collaboration between their intelligence agencies (CIA-ISI); and highlights the role of fundamentalist Islamic forces during the Afghan crisis.

As stated earlier, Pakistan's relationship with USA has been very complex. This tie-up started growing in the mid 1950s, particularly after the US pact when Islamabad became the principal ally of Washington in South Asia. US was interested in developing a close alliance with Pakistan especially after the crisis of its strategy in the oil bearing region of West-Asia. But this relationship did not develop in a straight line, and this changed with the changing perception of the American military strategy for Asia. (Chopra, V.D. "Pentagon Shadow over India" (Patriot pub, 1985, pp. 170-172).

US-Pakistan security relations were partial. From the indepandance but for the United States, the Soviet Union remains more important than Pakistan itself, India remains the chief security threat and these threats overshadow relations with both the United States and Soviet Union. The overall US-Pakistan security relationship is thus forever subject to buffeting by the other relationships and events.

Security relations between the two states are asymmetrical. The relationship has been, and may remain more important to Pakistan than to the United States. The latter's involvement in South Asia has been intermittent and it can withdraw from the region with little loss. Pakistan cannot withdraw; it's very survival is continuously at stake;

The security interest of the two states are non-congruent for Pakistan, the US represents an important source of weapons and political support useful in a whole range of diplomatic and military fronts. For the United States, Pakistan's position acts as a counter to the Soviet Union that makes it important, and; the security relationship remains burdened by an extreme degree of distortion, misperception and stereo types on both sides.

American still see Pakistan as everything from a nation of "little brown brothers" staunchly defending the ramparts of the free world against communist onslaughts, to a nation run by crazed religious fanatics. Pakistanis see the United States as alternatively omnipotent and incompetent in addressing its own vital affairs. From its very inception, Pakistan's foreign policy has been based on anti-India tirade. It will be more correct to say that Pakistani's world outlook was determined by its relationship with India. One of the most important reasons behind Pakistan's joining of western military alliances had been to achieve parity with India especially in the military field. (Leo, E.Rose and Noor A. Hussain, 1987, pp.15-16). Other forces which seemed to draw Pakistan towards the west were the elite in Pakistan drawn mainly from the feudal and military classes trained in western education and the political instability in Pakistan. The relationship between United States and the Pakistan is unique in many ways.

During the Cold War and the security fears that it induced demanded that American officials first identify and classify with sonnet precision the major elements of interest for the United States in every region of the globe. They needed to define the complex nix of strategic, economic, and political interests that South Asia held for the United States before they could agree upon what tactics were best designed to secure those interests. The most fundamental issue, then, involved discerning the overall value, marked or covert, of an area situated far from the major theatres of Cold War conflict. (McMahon, p.12)

The US-Pakistan strategic relationship are based on the shared interests between them in building a stable and sustainable democracy and in promoting peace, security, stability, prosperity, and democracy in South Asia and across the globe. (http://www.fact Sheet United States and Pakistan Long-Term Strategic Partners.htm).The US policy towards Pakistan was a historical object of the "pact mania" strategy that characterised the 1950s. American officials originally envisioned Pakistan as merely one member of the Baghdad Pact, a multilateral alliance on the southern flank of the USSR designed to thwart any expansionist goals in that direction. The Baghdad pact suffered a severe blow almost immediately when Iraq withdrew following an anti- western revolution in 1958. Turkey increasingly gravitated towards its association with Western Europe through NATO, showing only modest interest in South Asian problems. The United States moved quickly to fill at least part of the void through bilateral arrangements with both Pakistan and Iran, but that approach also collapsed following the 1979 Iranian revolution. Only Pakistan continues to fulfil its assigned role as a US sponsored guard in South Asia, and it was far too weak to bear such an enormous burden. The strategic cooperation between the United States and Pakistan were symbolised by a security agreement concluded in 1959, but the relationship was far more comprehensive. The United States has provided more than five billion dollars in economic and military aid since the mid-1950s. Pakistan's armed forces, 12th largest in the world, are equipped with an array of modern weapons, courtesy of the American treasury. A succession of governments in Islamabad has rewarded this generosity by consistently supporting US foreign policy positions by most Third World states. (Shirin, Tahir-Kheli, 1982, pp. 6-10).

The US-Pakistan connection has survived a host of difficulties. India's supporters in the United States have long contended that support for Pakistan needlessly drives a wedge between this country and the world's most populous democracy. Such critics repeatedly advise American officials to recognise that India inevitably the dominant power on the subcontinent, and they recommend that US policy be adjusted to reflect that reality.

While this view has attracted several adherents over the years, including John Kenneth Galbraith, Chester Bowles, and at least during his Senate career, John F Kennedy, its impact on US policy has been limited. Pressure from pro-India forces did impel President Lyndon Johnson to embargo arms aid to Pakistan during the 1965 Indo-Pakistan conflict, when it became evident that Pakistan had violated restrictions on the assistance by using US-supplied weapons for aggressive purposes. Similar lobbying contributed to a decision by the Carter administration to suspend economic and military assistance because of Pakistan's surreptitious military nuclear programme. But the basic features of a close US-Pakistan relationship have survived such setbacks. A succession of American administrations have stressed the importance of political and military ties with Islamabad even when this position severely strained relations with New Delhi and contributed to growing Indo-Soviet cooperation. The pro-Pakistan orientation culminated in President Nixon's famous "tilt" towards Pakistan during that country's 1971 war with India. (Kissinger, Henry, 1979, pp. 842-9182)

The relationship had also surmounted a series of unpalatable developments within Pakistan. US officials are often discomfited that our South Asian ally has been dominated by a series of military dictatorships, an embarrassing contrast to India's history. Civilian rule had accounted for barely one third of Pakistan's four decades of independence. Moreover, these dictatorial regimes have amassed a distressing record of human rights violations. Endemic political instability in Pakistan has also strained the relationship with Washington. The 1971 "tilt" occurred in the aftermath of a bloody civil war in which East Pakistan broke away to form the new nation of Bangladesh. During the mid-1970s, the government in Islamabad fought a lengthy and difficult campaign to suppress another separatist movement in Baluchistan province. Other secessionist impulses, while less potent, have surfaced repeatedly throughout the country's troubled history.

A continuing source of alarm for the United States was Pakistan's apparent determination to develop a military nuclear capability to match a similar programme in India. Not only does this strategy undermine Washington's long-standing effort to prevent the proliferation of nuclear weapons, it creates undesirable risks for the United States. American policy-makers exhibit understandable uneasiness about Pakistan obtaining nuclear armaments given that country's exceedingly stormy relationship with India. (Washington Post, November 9, 1986).Such ominous developments should have caused US policy-makers to reassess the wisdom of investing so much diplomatic, political, and military capital in an unpredictable and unstable ally. For a brief period during the early years of the Carter administration there was some evidence of a revaluation, but any inclination to deemphasise the Pakistan connection vanished when Soviet troops invaded Afghanistan. The Carter administration promptly muted its criticism of the Zia regime's human rights record, reiterated the 1959 security guarantee, and offered a new package of military aid totalling some $400 million. (Foreign Affairs, 1986, pp. 1026-1047). In the 1980s, we cooperated to resist the Soviet advance in Afghanistan. As a result, we helped the consolidation of freedom movements in Eastern Europe and hastened the end of the Cold War, bringing about the momentous transformation of our time. The lesson was clear that Pakistan-US relations have strategic character. Pakistan was pivotal to a sensitive region where the United States and the rest of the world have important interests at stake. The stability of the region demands a positive and constructive longterm relationship between our two countries. (http://www.heritage.org/Research/Asiaand the Pacific/hl929.cfm).

New US president Ronald Reagan had promised higher defence expenditures and a more vigorous foreign policy in response to Soviet advances in the Third World. High on the new administration's national security agenda was forging a closer relationship with Pakistan. Regarding the former ally as a potentially key partner in opposing the Soviet military presence in Afghanistan, Reagan and his top foreign policy aides, Secretary of State Alexander Haig, Director of Central Intelligence William Casey, and Secretary of Defence Caspar Weinberger, believed that Pakistan deserved far more US support than Carter had offered. (Kux, p. 256).During the intervening years, Pakistan has resumed its traditional role as America's principal political and military outpost in South Asia. Congress authorised a $3.2 billion five-year aid package in 1981, and the Reagan administration requested a new programme exceeding $4 billion when the original measure expired at the end of 1987. In exchange, Washington pressured the Zia government to serve as a conduit for covert US military aid to Afghan rebel forces–the Mujahidin fighting the Soviet occupation army. That assistance was estimated at $250-$300 million annually. The direct aid to Pakistan (which has included F-16 fighters and other sophisticated weapons in the American arsenal normally not available to Third World allies) combined with Islamabad's heightened role in the Afghanistan conflict underscores how much the United States has invested in its South Asian policy. Evidence suggests, however, that it is a risky and unwise commitment.

Washington views Pakistan both as a bulwark in its own right against Soviet expansion and as an important component of American policy towards Afghanistan. But Pakistan was an extraordinarily physical weak within ally- an impoverished nation with a history of political separatism and instability, governed precariously by a military strongman who faces mounting domestic opposition. The last point was underscored in April 1986 when massive anti-government crowds greeted the return from exile of Benazir Bhutto, daughter of the country's last elected prime minister and heir to his political machine. Pakistan seems destined for yet another period of angry and full of bitter words acrimonious confrontation and domestic turmoil. By placing so much reliance on a weak and unstable ally, the United States risks the collapse of its entire South Asian policy.

For a time, this confrontational strategy seemed to work. It gradually became evident, however, that Bhutto overestimated both the breadth of public dissatisfaction with the Zia regime and the depth of allegiance to her. Calls for massive demonstrations in July on the ninth anniversary of Zia's coup against her father resulted in disappointing turnouts. Ignoring this warning that she might be overreaching herself, Bhutto and her organisation again took to the streets the following month. This time there were continuous, sizable demonstrations in her home province of Sind, but elsewhere the initial outpouring of support quickly evaporated. Moreover, the government of Zia's hand-picked Prime Minister, Mohammad Khan Junejo, responded to the provocations by declaring a state of emergency and jailing Bhutto and hundreds of her followers. (Newsweek, August 25, 1986, p. 41) This crackdown marked a reversal of hesitant but encouraging steps towards democracy, including the election of a "nonpartisan" parliament in 1985 and the legalisation of political parties in early 1986.

Benazir Bhutto had openly tried to duplicate the successful revolution led by Corazon Aquino in the Philippines. It was an image she evoked in most of her speeches, and the Western news media were quick to proclaim "parallels" between the Philippine and Pakistan struggles (Newsweek, July 7, 1986, pp. 33-35). But by the autumn of 1986 one extremely clear difference had emerged - While Aquino had swept Into office amidst the acclaim of a decisive majority of her countrymen, Bhutto failed in her initial bid for power.

The divergent results should not had been so surprising to Western observers. So-called parallels with the Philippine revolution are vastly overdrawn. While some similarities do exist, there are also crucial differences. The United States should not expect a bloodless transfer of power to a democratic, pro-Western government. Pakistan's history and the dynamics of the current political environment suggest a less appealing outcome. Indeed, the personalised struggle between President Zia and his challenger often obscures more fundamental problems that, quite literally, threaten to unravel Pakistan as a nation-state. It was acuite.

While most experts concluded that the aloof Mohammad Zia-ul-Haq would encounter difficulty winning a fair election especially against a charismatic opponent such as Benazir Bhutto he is much stronger politically than Ferdinand Marcos. One crucial difference is the attitude of the nation's clergy. In marked contrast, the bulk of Pakistan's Islamic clergy seems solidly pro-government. This stance is largely a consequence of President Zia's "Islamisation" campaign during the early 1980s to make Pakistani criminal and civil law conform to the dictates of the Quran. While the subsequent changes were more cosmetic than substantive, they represented a significant symbolic victory for Islamic fundamentalists. (Foreign Policy, Summer-1985, pp. 161-162) Zia thereby neutralised a potentially dangerous source of opposition to his regime.

The future of Pakistan would be problematic even under the most favourable conditions. US foreign policy objectives in South Asia, and the resulting demands placed upon Pakistan as the principal American client in the region, are greatly magnifying the danger. Unless Washington pursues a more perceptive strategy, it courts disaster both for itself and its long time ally.

The Afghanistan conflict has not only given Pakistan an unwanted Soviet neighbour, but has also created a new and very serious burden on the nation's fragile social structure. More than three million Afghan refugees now live in camps along the border, primarily in Baluchistan and the Nuclear Weapon Free Zone (NWFZ). In addition, thousands of armed Mujahidin utilise Pakistani territory as a base for military operations against the Soviets inside Afghanistan.

Initially, the Pakistani people appeared to support that position overwhelmingly. But as the Afghan war enters its eighth year, the refugee numbers continue to mount, and Islamabad's support for the Mujahidin raises the spectre of a military clash with the USSR, the consensus has fragmented.

Critics cite the $1 million per day cost to the national treasury to feed and shelter the refugees. They also contend that the Afghans strain already overburdened public services (especially water supplies), compete "unfairly" with Pakistanis for jobs, and contribute to growing crime problems. (New York Times, October 17) Hostility is most evident in Baluchistan, but complaints against the Afghans are mounting even among their Pushtun ethnic brethren in the NWFP. Discontent throughout the country was sufficiently strong that opponents of the Zia government have made the refugee problem a major issue, calling for Pakistan to break with the United States and seek a compromise solution to the war in Afghanistan. (Ayoob, pp. 164-172)

US wanted to make Pakistan the chief American client in the region and a pawn in the superpower rivalry with the Soviet Union extremely unadvisable (Foreign Policy, 1980, pp. 35-51). Pakistan was an ally afflicted with numerous separatist forces, facing powerful, hostile neighbours on two sides, and confronting an increasingly divisive refugee presence. This refugee issue the newest ingredient in an already explosive mixture should not be under-estimated. The current situation in Pakistan bears an alarming resemblance to conditions in Lebanon during the early and mid-1970s.

Pakistan would be fortunate if it survive as a political entity in the coming years. The country faces a host of daunting difficulties, and US policy in South Asia makes them significantly worse. Washington's desired for a reliable ally was creating serious dangers both for Pakistan and the United States.

The Reagan administration's decision to give Pakistan advanced weaponry, including 40 F-16 fighters, had especially angered Mrs Gandhi government. While the United States insisted that this assistance is designed to bolster Pakistan's ability to defend itself from Soviet aggression, India not surprisingly adopts a different view, noting the three wars it has fought with its neighbour. Clearly, the Pakistani arsenal could be used against India in some future conflict. US military aid thus heightens Indian hostility towards Pakistan as well as poisoning Indo-American relations. (Foreign Policy, 1986, pp. 148-166) It also gave India and the Soviet Union a common focal point for their foreign policy concerns, thus helping to cement an otherwise curious alliance between a democracy and the world's most notorious totalitarian state.

US wanted to stablise military and political base in South Asia places Pakistan on the frontlines in an ongoing superpower struggle. This causes the Kremlin to pay an inordinate amount of attention to an otherwise relatively minor Third World country. Moscow had an obvious incentive to eliminate a US ally on its geopolitical doorstep, either through military intimidation or attempts at destabilisation.

The Soviets union cultivated extensive contacts with Baluchistan separatist leaders for many years and apparently provided modest clandestine aid to the rebels during the uprising in the 1970s. There were indications as well that Moscow maintains contact with left-wing elements in the anti-Zia coalition. While such subversive activities have thus far remained at relatively low levels, the infrastructure for a more concerted campaign was built.

Pakistan was the main channel for US military assistance to the Afghan Mujahedin exposes that nation to especially grave risks. The USSR obviously regards Afghanistan as a high-priority foreign policy concern. Moscow would scarcely have destroyed detente with the United States and committed 120,000 troops to a seemingly endless war if this were not the case. Therefore, the Kremlin leaders are likely to regard joint US-Pakistani assistance to the Afghan rebels as a serious threat to its interests. The Red Army's inability to crush the insurgency and restore stability to Afghanistan on communist terms creates an additional incentive to cut the Gordian knot in some other way. Since the soviets could not strike directly at its superpower rival without risking a global conflagration, the most feasible strategy increased political and military pressure on the more vulnerable antagonist–Pakistan.

And then the most obvious and most probable threat comes form Soviet subversion activities, but an even more ominous danger exists. If the Afghan stalemate continues, and especially if the Mujahidin seem poised to topple the Kabul regime despite Soviet military assistance, Moscow will be tempted to strike directly at the sanctuaries across the border in Pakistan. There had already been dozens of "minor" incidents this year, primarily cross-border shelling and intrusions into Pakistani air space by communist (Soviet and Afghan) planes. Although such episodes thus far seem to constitute more a "war of nerves" than a harbinger of a general offensive, it is disquieting that both the number and severity of incidents have increased from previous years. (New York Times, October 30, 1986) Soviet protests to Islamabad concerning the use of Pakistani territory as sanctuaries by the Mujahidin had also become noticeably more strident in recent months.

Moscow attempted wipe out those refugees or even adopt a limited "hot pursuit" policy, it would created an extremely crucial situation. The Zia government would face an unpalatable choice. If it failed to respond to such blatant provocations, the government would be tacitly conceding an inability to defend the homeland. The Zia regime's already precarious position, such a humiliation might well topple it from power. The possibility of Soviet military pressure on Pakistan not only imperils that country, it poses serious risks for the United States. The ongoing political and military association with Pakistan endangered for American security in three ways. 1st, Soviet move against the Afghan border sanctuaries would probably impel Islamabad to invoke the 1959 security pact, since it was extremely unlikely that the Pakistanis would take on the Red Army alone. In addition to the 1959 agreement, Washington strengthened its commitment following the invasion of Afghanistan by proclaiming the Carter Doctrine, pledging resistance to any further aggression towards the Persian Gulf-Indian Ocean region. US officials would therefore have to decide whether to dishonour those commitments or come to the aid of Pakistan even though it entailed a direct confrontation with the USSR. It was uncertain how effective American assistance might be given inherent geographic limitations. While the United States maintains a significant naval presence in the Indian Ocean and a rapid deployment force was explicitly created for possible use in this region, American military capabilities would be dwarfed by those of the USSR. The Soviets would be operating less than 1,000 miles away from their homeland; the United States more than 8,000. It was a sobering disparity. The 1959 security treaty was created at a time when the United States enjoyed a decisive edge in nuclear weaponry. Under those conditions, Washington could threaten (with reasonable credibility) a devastating response if Moscow dared attack Pakistan or any other American ally. In today's environment of strategic parity, such warnings possess little if any credibility. An obsolete security treaty thereby places the United States in a position of retaining a military obligation that it can no longer fulfil. A commitment so totally lacking in credibility virtually invites challenge.Even, if the United States managed to avoid the nightmare of a military confrontation with the Soviet Union in South Asia, the Pakistani connection involved another risk. The same security agreement that Islamabad could invoke against a Soviet attack, it might attempt to employ in the event of a new Indo-Pakistani war. While the treaty applied explicitly to communist aggression, the close association between India and the USSR makes that point disturbingly ambiguous. The Zia government openly accused India of being an undeclared Russian ally and might have well argued that an attack from that quarter constituted a Soviet-orchestrated threat. It should be noted that the government of Pakistan attempted a similar scheme in the 1971 war, at a time when Indo-Soviet cooperation was considerably less extensive (Kissinger, pp. 894-895).

Washington would probably rejected such a claim, but the danger of a clash with India could come in other ways. Pakistan would certainly employ its modern American-made weapons in the event of war. However, much US leaders might object. Moreover, the United States would face a terrible dilemma if the war began to go badly for Pakistan, a distinct possibility, given the disparity in population and military capabilities between the two powers. Unless Indian objectives remained extremely limited, a Pakistani defeat might involve irreparable damage to that country as a political entity. There would exist considerable pressure on American officials to prevent that outcome, even if it meant risking a military clash with India. It was indicative of the tension on this score between New Delhi and Washington that Indian public opinion increasingly regards a military conflict with the United States as a serious possibility. (Harrison, pp. 126-127)

The possible consequences of American involvement in a new war between Pakistan and India must be assessed against the backdrop of nuclear weapons development in both countries. India demonstrated its capability by detonating to explode an atomic device in 1974, and rumours abound that New Delhi now possessed a small arsenal. The Zia government insists officially that Pakistan has no nuclear weapons programme, but this denial possesses meagre credibility either inside or outside the country. Prudence dictates that the United States must operate on the assumption that both nations were,or shortly will be nuclear powers. Given the record of conflict since partition and the continuing tense state of Indo-Pakistani relations, that probability underscores how dangerous our political and military association with Pakistan has become.

The prospect of war was certainly the most serious problem, but the United States was incurring another risk. Washington has built an elaborate geopolitical strategy in South Asia, assuming an obligation to keep the Persian Gulf oil routes open and escalating assistance to the rebels in Afghanistan. Crucial to this regional policy was the continuation of Pakistan as an effective political and military ally. The loss of Pakistan, either through external pressure or domestic turmoil, would literally destroy the entire foundation for American policy in South Asia. By basing its strategy so totally on a weak and unstable ally, the United States risks creating regional chaos and probably an irresistible opportunity for Soviet expansionism precisely what Washington has fought to prevent for more than three decades. While it may seem paradoxical to some observers, the preservation (or more accurately, the creation) of a stable, non-communist barrier to Soviet expansion in South Asia requires US military disengagement from the region and an end to the Pakistani connection.

Although Pakistan assuredly wanted to retain the apparent military protection afforded by its security treaty with the United States, there were also signs that Islamabad was beginning to recognise some of the dangers involved in being America's client. Despite Pakistan was receiving more than $600 million doller per year from US, the Zia government increasingly began resisting US demands. The most obvious examples of tension occurred with reference to policy towards Afghanistan.

Pakistan has never been entirely comfortable in its role as a conduit for American military aid to the Mujahidin. Rebel leaders have complained for years that equipment destined for their forces gets delayed or even siphoned off by Pakistani officials. Most recently, there have been loud objections that sophisticated weapons such as the shoulder launched "Stinger" ground-to-air missiles are being intercepted.

Moreover, Pakistan's leaders were nervous about arming powerful Mujahidin units which they cannot control. President Zia served as an official attached to the embassy in Jordan in 1969 and 1970 when King Hussein found his power severely eroded by the PLO, and this experience apparently made an indelible impression. Zia understood how perilous it could be to his political fortunes to have a well-armed foreign guerrilla army operating in his country. (Ayoob, pp. 166-167) Despite intense US pressure to assist the Mujahidin and the pull of religious solidarity. The Zia government regarded its role with mounting apprehension.

Pakistan adopted a different view and it had been an active participant in UN-sponsored negotiations since their inception in 1982. While Islamabad insisted upon a definite time- table for the withdrawal of Soviet troops, it has displayed a willingness to discuss various compromise measures. In marked contrast to the US insistence that the Mujahidin be a party to negotiations for a settlement of the Afghan conflict, Pakistan would seem to prefer direct talks between Islamabad and Kabul assuming the Soviet troop withdrawal problem could be overcome. These disagreements have been an increasing source of tension between the United States and Pakistan. (Ziring, 1983, pp. 39-54)

The Reagan administration was using Afghanistan as a testing ground for the so-called Reagan Doctrine of providing aid to anti-Soviet insurgents in the Third World. It also seems content to use the Mujahidin to tie down Soviet military forces in a bloody, protracted conflict.

The Pakistani government, however, worries about the massive Afghan presence in its country and the burden placed on an already fragile domestic, social and political structure. Pakistani officials have a much greater incentive to seek a compromise solution, even if that must come at the expense of the insurgents. They want a settlement, above all, that reduces the Soviet military threat on Pakistan's border and enables the Afghan refugees to go home.

If the Reagan administration found the Zia government to be an increasingly reluctant and recalcitrant ally, it would be even less happy should the opposition come to power. The Pakistan People's Party explicitly advocated a non-aligned foreign policy and excoriated Zia for doing Washington's bidding in South Asia. Bhutto and her followers made it clear that they would not allow their country to be used as a sanctuary for the Afghan insurgents nor would Pakistan continue as a distributor for US arms destined for the Mujahidin (Ayoob, p. 172). A significant faction within the other principal opposition group, the MRD, was even more virulently anti-American, routinely denouncing the Zia regime as an instrument of "US imperialism". Given the growing public concern about the presence of the Afghan refugees and danger of a military clash with the USSR, the anti-Zia forces sensed that they had a popular issue.

The incumbent government's cautious but visible attempts to distance itself from the more doctrinaire aspects of US policy suggested that this perception was correct. It raised yet another question about Pakistan's reliability as an ally.

While the US objective of preventing Soviet expansionism in South Asia might be admirable in the abstract, it had no connection to current realities. Pakistan's ability to constrain the USSR directly was severely limited. The Soviets could bring their military power to bear in that region far more easily than could a rival located on the other side of the globe. Unless the United States was willing to risk a nuclear conflagration, there was no effective way to neutralise that geographic advantage. Moreover, contrary to the hysteria surrounding the promulgation of the Carter Doctrine, there was nothing in South Asia not even the much-touted Persian Gulf oil routes worthy of incurring such a grave risk.

If American policy-makers truly believe that a stable, non-communist Pakistan constitutes an essential barrier to Soviet expansionism, then a drastic reorientation of US policy is essential.

Pakistan should immediately realise the adversities of its large scale involvement in military activities and begin to stabilise its economy. Pakistan badly needs to implement internal political and economic reforms if it was to survive as a nation. Politically, a democratic system based on federalist principles constitutes the most feasible mechanism for peaceful change, while recognising the great diversity of the various provinces. It offers at least some hope of defusing the endemic ethnic and regional separatist pressures.

Economic reforms are equally essential. On the way out economy is a virtual invitation for social and political turmoil. Pakistan needs to pursue even more aggressively than the Zia's government has done thus far-measures aimed at cutting away the stifling web of state socialism. The creation of a market economy will enable Pakistan to join the ranks of other non-communist Asian nations such as Thailand and Malaysia that have experienced rapid economic growth in the past two decades.

A more hospitable external environment would greatly facilitate Pakistan's ability to implement such reforms. One crucial feature of that environment was diminished Soviet and Indian hostility, but such a change was unlikely to occur so long as Pakistan remained a US political and military ally. Quite the contrary, pressure from Moscow and New Delhi would probably intensify as the USSR pursued an elusive victory in Afghanistan and India fretted about having a neighbour armed with nuclear weapons serving as a surrogate for American power.

Using Pakistan as a pawn not only helped create powerful foreign enemies for that country, it was exacerbating the already formidable domestic strains. The vast quantities of American military aid since the 1950s had greatly strengthened the Pakistani military at the expense of the civilian sector. This had both weakened democratic elements and distorted the economy, gearing it towards a garrison state rather than consumer production. Washington's uncritical support for the current "friendly" autocratic government (as well as its predecessors) antagonised competing political elements and strengthens separatist forces that saw no hope for change within Pakistan. Finally, employing Pakistan as an instrument for carrying out US policy in Afghanistan had brought to the fore a new divisive Issue, thereby creating even more political and social instability. It was in all respects a dangerous and narrow-minded strategy.

The crucial feature of a new US policy in South Asia was the severing of extensive political and military ties with Pakistan. This implied not only abrogation of the security agreement, but the termination of military and economic aid programmes and an end to using the country as a conduit for assisting the Afghan rebels. In short, it necessitated military disengagement from South Asia and a much lower political profile.

Without the protection of its superpower patron, Pakistan might also fall victim to Indian hegemonic aspirations. Certainly the religious animosity, the territorial dispute involving Kashmir, and the suspicions concerning rival nuclear weapons programmes would not disappear overnight.

Any one of those issues could ignite a fourth Indo-Pakistani war, and without American military aid a decisive Indian victory would be almost certain. Although some danger existed that Moscow or New Delhi might respond to a US military withdrawal from South Asia by crushing Pakistan, there was ample reason to expect a more peaceful aftermath. The Soviets in particular would pay an exceedingly high price if they moved to establish their power on the shores of the Indian Ocean. Soviet policy-makers had spent three decades cultivating close ties with India. Although this policy had been quite successful, it was significant that a discernible cooling of relations had taken place as the Soviet occupation of Afghanistan dragged into its eighth year. It was extremely doubtful whether the Mrs Gandhi government could regarded a Sovietised Pakistan- a development that would place the Red Army on India's border along a thousand-mile front as anything other than a menace to national security. In short, the USSR could achieve its coveted warm water ports only at a grave risk to its relationship with India an association Moscow considers vital to counter Chinese power. It was unlikely that the Kremlin leaders would be willing to pay such an exorbitant price. Pakistan, therefore, represented an important buffer between Soviet and Indian spheres of influence. This realisation would probably inhibit New Delhi from precipitous action just as it would Moscow.

Even if Pakistan avoided external calamities, severe internal political and economic difficulties would remain. The struggle between conservative forces supporting the government and the coalition of moderate and radical opposition elements was unlikely to dissipate. Similarly, neither the Sind-Punjab rivalry nor the powerful separatist campaigns (especially in Baluchistan) would soon vanish. The Pakistani people might have the foresight to enact the political and economic reforms needed to avert catastrophe, but they might also refuse to take those steps, or at least fail to do so in time. Even under the best of conditions, Pakistan's continued survival could not be guaranteed. The presence of risks should not obscure the fact that the opportunity for a benign solution also exists. Indeed, if the United States pursued a sophisticated disengagement strategy, it might help transform much of South Asia into an island of stability while defusing a possible source of conflict with the Soviet Union.

There were subtle but significant signs that the Soviets were becoming weary of their military involvement in Afghanistan. General Secretary Gorbachev's admission that Afghanistan had become "a bleeding wound" was merely one of several indicators. At the same time, Moscow adamantly refused to withdraw from that country in a manner that appeared to give the United States a major propaganda and geopolitical triumph. Rather than accepting such a humiliating setback, the Soviets would probably fight on indefinitely. The Mujahidin, for all their bravery, would not be able to dislodge a determined occupation by the Red Army, although they could continue to make it a costly and bloody one. US policy-makers had the opportunity to offer the Soviet Union an extremely tempting package deal. The arrangement would involve an "Austrian solution" for both Afghanistan and Pakistan.

Frontline State

The United States, which was initially unresponsive to their importunities, gradually became interested in "using" Pakistan for purposes that it deemed important for its own security objectives (Venkatramni, p. xi).

The Soviet invasion in Afghanistan had made Pakistan a country of top geo-strategic importance for the United States. The United States declared that Pakistan is a "frontline state" against Soviet aggression and offered to regenerate aid and military assistance deliveries. For the remainder of Zia's tenure, the United States generally ignored Pakistan's developing nuclear programme. Other donors also rallied to Pakistan as it stood firm against the Soviet blustering hospitably and received over three million Afghan refugees who poured across the borders. This provided a conduit for weapons and other support, and gave a safe haven to the Afghan Mujahidin. Pakistan's top national security agency, the army's Directorate for Inter-Services Intelligence, monitored the activities of and provided advice and support to the Mujahidin, and commandos from the army's Special Services Group helped guide the operations inside Afghanistan. In the Muslim world, Pakistan increasingly assumed a leading role. As a long-term goal, Zia predicted the emergence of an Islamic government in Kabul that would provide Pakistan with geo-strategic depth, facilitate access to Muslim West Asia, and forswear a revision of the Pakistan-Afghanistan boundary.

Pakistan paid a price for its activities. The refugee burden, even if offset in part by foreign assistance, created dangerous pressures within Pakistani society. Afghan and Soviet forces raided against Mujahidin bases inside Pakistan, and a campaign of terror bombings and sabotage in Pakistan's cities guided by Afghan intelligence agents caused hundreds of casualties. There is no concrete evidence to support the revitalised "Great Game" argument that the Soviet invasion was a modern manifestation of Russia's historic drive to garner access to a warm water port and that it was but a first step on a road through Pakistan to the Arabian Sea. Nor was it likely that the Soviet Union would have conducted major military operations against Pakistan as long as Islamabad did not flaunt its support to the Mujahidin.

Zia's ability to obtain high levels of support and modern weaponry strengthened his position within the military establishment and enabled Pakistan once again to build up a credible military capability. Under the United States assistance programme, Pakistan bought F-16 aircrafts, upgraded M-48 tanks, Harpoon naval missiles, helicopters, and artillery, and received second-hand frigates on loan. In the four years after the invasion, Pakistan's armed forces grew by nearly 12 per cent, from 428,000 to 478,000 persons. A substantial amount of the costs of modernisation and expansion were covered by United States aid and financial contributions from Saudi Arabia and Persian Gulf countries.

Zia was very clever at protecting his base in the military and ensured United Stated to control it. At the same time as the chief of the army staff, chief martial law administrator, and president, he carefully managed senior military appointments. The satisfaction of the military was also enhanced by arrangements under which Pakistani service personnel were seconded to the armed forces of Persian Gulf countries, where emoluments were much more generous than in Pakistan. Retiring officers received generous benefits, sometimes including land allocations. They repeatedly found themselves in profitable positions in government service or in parastatal economic enterprises. The assignment of serving officers to approximately 10 per cent of the senior posts in the civilian administration also provided opportunities for economic gain, sometimes in ways that were ultimately harmful to the army's image of itself.

Zia had learned the lesson of 1965 well, and was careful not to allow the nation to return to the status of a client state of the United States. Even as Pakistan faced the Soviet Union in Afghanistan, it kept that threat in perspective. Immediately after the Soviet invasion of Afghanistan in December 1979, Zia declined the Carter administration's assistance package offer of US$ 400 million as "peanuts." It was not until 1981 that Pakistan concluded an assistance agreement with the United States, which provided for US$ 3.2 billion over six years, divided equally between economic and military aid. This agreement was extended in 1986 to provide an additional US$ 4.0 billion over the next six years. (http://www.country-data.com/cgi-bin/query/r-9901.html)

During the Soviet invasion of Afghanistan in December 1979, Pakistan was again viewed as a frontline state against Soviet expansionism. An offer to Pakistan of US$ 400 million in economic and security aid by the Carter Administration in early 1980 was turned down by President Zia-ul-Haq as "peanuts." In September 1981, however, the Reagan Administration negotiated a US$ 3.2 billion, five-year economic and military aid package with Pakistan. Congress facilitated the resumption of aid in December by adding Section 620E to the FAA, giving the President authority to waive Section 669 for six years in the case of Pakistan, on grounds of national interest. Pakistan became a funnel for arms supplies to the Afghan resistance, as well as a camp for three million Afghan refugees. Despite the renewal of US aid and close security ties, many in Congress remained concerned about Pakistan's nuclear programme, based, in part, on evidence of US export control violations that suggested a crash programme to acquire a nuclear weapons capability. In 1985, Section 620E(e) (so-called Pressler Amendment) was added to the FAA, requiring the President to certify to Congress that Pakistan does not possess a nuclear explosive device during the fiscal year for which aid is to be provided. The Pressler amendment represented a compromise between those in Congress who thought that aid to Pakistan should be cut off because of evidence that it was continuing to develop its nuclear option and those who favoured continued support for Pakistan's role in opposing Soviet occupation of Afghanistan. A US$ 4 billion, six-year aid package for Pakistan was signed in 1986. (*CRS*, 15, 2001, pp.1-2)

Zia's policies inevitably led to a worsening of relations with India, which was disturbed by the reentry of the United States into the South Asian security equation, and by what India saw as the impetus to a new arms race. India responded with large-scale arms purchases of its own, primarily from the Soviet Union, which more than matched anything that the United States provided to Pakistan. Zia took considerable pains to reduce tensions and launched several peace initiatives, which New Delhi, however, failed to accept. Whether Zia saw his own efforts merely as diplomatic manoeuvres was unclear, but they reflected a growing realisation in Pakistan that unconstrained enmity with India was simply too dangerous and beyond Pakistan's means.

There were periods of considerable tension between Pakistan and India. In November 1986, India launched its largest manoeuvre ever, Operation Brass Tacks, menacingly close to the Pakistan border. The Pakistan Army responded with threatening counter movements, and in early 1987 there was serious concern that a war might break out. The India-Pakistan hotline was brought into use, and Zia skilfully seized the initiative by travelling to India to view a cricket game, using the opportunity to meet with Indian leaders to defuse the situation.

Among the major disputes between these two countries, only that over the Siachen Glacier, which is located in a remote area of northern Kashmir where boundaries are ill defined, has led to fighting in recent years. The two armies had been in desultory but very costly (primarily because of exposure to the elements) high-altitude combat there since 1984, when Indian forces moved into previously unoccupied territory at the extreme northern end of the Kashmir Line of Control.

Aside from Afghanistan, the most problematic element in Pakistan's security policy was the nuclear question. Zia inherited an ambitious programme from Bhutto and continued to develop it, out of the realisation that, despite Pakistan's newly acquired weaponry, it could never match India's conventional power and that India either had, or shortly could develop, its own nuclear weapons. Even after the invasion of Afghanistan, Pakistan almost exhausted United State's tolerance, including bungled attempts to illegally acquire United States nuclear-relevant technology and a virtual public admission in 1987 by the head of Pakistan's nuclear programme that the country had developed a weapon. As long as Pakistan remained vital to United States' interests in Afghanistan, however, no action was taken to cut off United States support. Pakistani attempts to handle the problem bilaterally with India led nowhere, but a significant step was a non-formalised 1985 agreement that neither India nor Pakistan would attack the other's nuclear facilities.

Zia showed a remarkable ability to keep himself in power, to promote Pakistan's international position, and to bring a modest degree of economic prosperity to Pakistan. His problem was how to devolve power. Beginning in 1985, a process of demilitarisation of the regime was launched, and Zia was elected civilian president of Pakistan through some highly dubious manoeuvring. In late 1985, he ended martial law and revised the 1973 constitution in ways that legitimised all actions taken by the martial law government since 1977, and strengthened his position as president. Mohammad Khan Junejo, whom Zia appointed prime minister in March 1985, managed to develop some degree of autonomy from Zia and persuaded him to allow political parties to reform; Junejo also watered down some of Zia's constitutional proposals, notably blocking the creation of the National Security Council-that would have institutionalised the role of the military.

The experiment in controlled democracy floundered in May 1988, when Zia abruptly dismissed the Junejo government for reasons that were not altogether clear but might have involved Junejo's attempt to gain a voice in security matters. Zia promised new elections, but most observers assumed that he would once again postpone them rather than take the risk that Benazir Bhutto, Zulfiqar's daughter, who had returned from exile abroad to a tumultuous welcome in Pakistan in 1986, would come to power. Benazir's programme included revenge for her father's death and punishment of Zia for staging the 1977 coup, which, under the 1973 constitution, rendered him liable to the death sentence. The crisis facing Pakistan resolved itself suddenly, however, when Zia was killed in a mysterious airplane crash in August 1988. Ghulam Ishaq Khan, a senior bureaucrat who was president of the Senate, succeeded to the presidency, and after consultations with the new chief of the army staff, General Mirza Aslam Beg, rather surprisingly decided to let the elections proceed as scheduled. (http://www.country-data.com/cgi-bin/query/r- 9901.html)

Massive Military and Economic Assistance

The root causes of Pakistan's economic and political woes

lie in its feudal society and the winner-take-all approach to governing that has been practised by successive civilian and military leaders. The party that brought Pakistan independence, the Muslim League, lacked internal democracy. Once partition and statehood had been achieved, the League, dominated by upperclass landed gentry from the former United Provinces of British India, displayed very title interest in forging a state that would promote popular participation and equity. Although they sought to free the Muslims of South Asia from Hindu domination, Pakistan's leaders failed to address the new state's own ethnic diversity. This was a critical shortcoming, for contrary to the political rhetoric of Pakistan's founder, Mohammed Ali Jinnah, the region's Muslims never constituted an inchoate, monolithic nation. Instead, a variety of Muslim communities existed throughout British India, and these communities were ridden by sectarian, ethnic, and class cleavages. (http://www. zia-reagan 1.htm)

The US friendship translated into substantial military and economic assistance for Pakistan. And such aid further bolstered the prerogatives of Pakistan's military, thanks in part to the weaknesses of the country's civilian institutions. During the Cold War, the United States agreed to ignore Pakistan's internal arrangements as long as its ally remained staunchly anti-communist. Free from any American pressure to pursue domestic political reform, Pakistan's military and its conservative civil service skewed the nation's developmental priorities, privileged the military's own position, and did little to dismantle the country's feudalistic, non-egalitarian social structures. Unlike neighbouring India, for example, Pakistan never undertook even a modest programme of land reform. (http:// www. zia-reagan 2.htm)

The United States and Pakistan established diplomatic relations in 1947. The US agreement to provide economic and military assistance to Pakistan and the latter's partnership in the Baghdad Pact/CENTO and SEATO strengthened relations between the two nations. However, the US suspension of military assistance during the 1965 Indo-Pakistan war generated a widespread feeling in Pakistan that the United States was not a reliable ally. Even though the United States suspended military assistance to both countries involved in the conflict, the suspension of aid affected Pakistan much more severely. Gradually, relations improved and arms sales were renewed in 1975. Then, in April 1979, the United States cut off economic assistance to Pakistan, except food assistance, as required under the Symington Amendment to the Foreign Assistance Act of 1961, due to concerns about Pakistan's nuclear programme.

Since independence Pakistan had to depend on foreign assistance in its development efforts and to balance its international debt payments. In 1960, the World Bank organised the Aid-to-Pakistan Consortium to facilitate coordination among the major providers of international assistance.

Most aid was in the form of loans, although the proportion of grants increased from around 12 per cent in the late 1970s to around 25 per cent in the 1980s, mainly because of food aid and other funds directed towards Afghan refugees. (http://www.country-data.com/cgi-bin/query/r-9826.html)

The Soviet invasion of Afghanistan in December 1979 highlighted the common interest of Pakistan and the United States in peace and stability in South Asia. In 1981, the United States and Pakistan agreed on a US$ 3.2 billion military and economic assistance programme aimed at helping Pakistan deal with the heightened threat to security in the region and its economic development needs (http://www.Pakistan Facilities.htm). Recognising national security concerns and accepting Pakistan's assurances that it did not intend to construct a nuclear weapon, Congress waived restrictions (Symington Amendment) on military assistance to Pakistan. In March 1986, the two countries agreed on a second multi-year (FY 1988-93) US$ 4 billion economic development and security assistance programme. The United States has been a major provider of aid since independence and was the largest donor in the 1980s. (http://www.country-data.com/cgibin/ query/r-9826.html)

The United States sought to contain the Soviet Union, prevent its spread to southern Asia, and stop it from reaching the Arabian Sea. Pakistan at its creation was unable to do this. After a traumatic Partition and an early war with India, the Pakistani state and military institutions were in shambles. Pakistan had to govern two wings separated by a thousand miles of hostile India. By allying with Pakistan, the United States injected large amounts of economic aid and larger sums of military assistance into Pakistan. It buttressed the institutions of state power and even more it created a formidable Pakistani military. During these first decades, the United States was the lifeline to Pakistan. Without US diplomatic, military, and economic aid, Pakistan would have had great difficulties surviving. These early policies have had lasting impacts. The Pakistan military would have more resources and would be better trained than any other sector of Pakistani society. The relative power balance between civilians and the military was tilted in the military's favour and has remained there ever since.

Indo-Pakistani relations in the 1960s were troubled, when Pakistan believed that the United States would support it even if it pursued aggressive policies to attain regional objectives. When it sought to "unfreeze" the situation in the disputed territory of Jammu and Kashmir in 1965 by deploying guerrillas across the Ceasefire Line (CFL), it was ostracised by the United States. When it launched a conventional operation across the CFL (Operation Grand Slam), India responded by an armoured thrust at Lahore. Pakistan sought US assistance to the Indian attack, but the US supported an arms embargo against both countries. This embargo would more or less remain in place until the Ford administration. The US sought to prevent the acquisition of threatening military capabilities in Pakistan-threatening to its neighbours not the United States-by denying Pakistan sales of military equipment. Rather than lessening the Pakistani appetite for military capabilities, these policies merely diverted Pakistan to a different source. For a brief time in the 1960s, Pakistan had a modest arms relationship with the Soviet Union, but more significantly in the 1960s, Pakistan developed a much broader strategic relationship with China.

In attempting to shape Pakistani policy, the US pushed Pakistan into the arms of its Communist foes. Instead of changing Pakistani behaviour, US policy diminished US influence over Pakistan. This pattern-where US leverage against Pakistan, if used, is diminished-has been repeated several times since.

The 1971 Bangladesh War fundamentally shaped Pakistan's strategic thinking, casting a shadow up to the present. Pakistan's own mismanagement of the Bengali population in East Pakistan led to a crisis following elections in 1971. As the Bengali insurrection grew, Pakistan had greater and greater difficulty controlling the situation. Refugees spilled over the Indian border and India decided to support Bengali insurgents from Indian Territory. As the crisis mounted, India determined that only armed intervention would achieve its security objectives. As K. Subrahmanyam put it, the Bangladesh crisis presented India with "an opportunity the like of which will never come again". India's invasion (or "liberation," depending on which side of the border you are on) of Bangladesh dismembered Pakistan. Despite President Richard Nixon's "tilt" towards Pakistan during the crisis and the deployment of the USS Enterprise to the Bay of Bengal-Pakistan's US ally was unable to prevent Dhaka's fall.

In 1972, Zulfikar Ali Bhutto launched Pakistan's nuclear weapons development effort. But only after India conducted its "peaceful nuclear explosion" in 1974, did Pakistan dramatically escalate its efforts. The US alliance was tailored for extra regional threats- and US assurance messages were also directed at dangers beyond South Asia. Its inability to provide security against regional foes led Pakistan to develop its own capability to deter them. By the mid-1970s, the Sardar Mohammed Daoud government was playing a complicated game with Afghanistan's Communists. In 1978, Daoud lost and the Communists took control in Kabul. (http://www. Strategic Insights Dissuasion and Regional Allies - The C.htm). Indian Government expressed their concern over reports on the US plans to increase arms sales to Pakistan in the wake of Soviet invasion of Afghanistan. (New York Times, January 1, 1980)

President Carter said that the US would be in touch with other countries on forming consortium to supply of military and economic aid to Pakistan. (New York Times, January 8, 1980)

President Mohammed Zia-ul-Haq refused US$ 400 million aid which was offered by US and called it 'peanuts'; president Zia stated that Pakistan would not buy its security with US$ 400 million, he stressed need for 'moral help' to enable Pakistan to defend itself against new threat along its border with Afghanistan. (New York Times, January 18, 1980)

Carter Administration continued to insist on Pakistan aid package in congress even though President Zia had dismissed the US$ 400 million offer; Mr. Carter said that the package was viewed as only part of aid programme to Pakistan. (New York Times, January 19, 1980)

Among the priorities set by President Carter in his Message to the Congress State of Union were aid package for Pakistan and other steps to respond to Soviet intervention in Afghanistan. (New York Times, January 22, 1980)

Secretary of State Vance told in Senate's Foreign Relations Committee that Carter Administration would delay the submission of US$ 400 million aid package for Pakistan in the field of military and economic area. (*ibid*)

In an article highlighting the US policy on Pakistan, it was mentioned that US must ensure to renew economic and military aid to Pakistan and that it should not be considered by Pakistan as a sign of acquiescence in its development of nuclear weapons. (*ibid*)

European Economic Community agreed to provide a sum of US$ 20 million aid package to Pakistan for its help and cooperation to Afghan refugees (New York Times, January 25, 1980).

Ronald Reagan repeated his call for American arms sales to Pakistan (*ibid*).

Zbigniew Brzezinski, President Carter's National Security Adviser, was to head a diplomatic mission to Pakistan to help the plan of US$ 400 million aid package, the delegation included Deputy State Secretary - Warren Christopher; another delegation headed by Assistant Secretary of State David E McGiffert was to accompany the Brzezinski group. (New York Times, January 29, 1980)

Carter Administration planned to enter into a long-term military support to Pakistan and it planned to extend support beyond crisis caused by Soviet intervention in Afghanistan (New York Times, February 1, 1980).

President Carter's special envoy, Clark M Clifford, defended US plan for arms sales to Pakistan during meeting with Indian officials; and he was to signal to Moscow that the latter would encounter opposition of many leading countries in the world if it attempted to move into Pakistan. (New York Times, February 1, 1980)

Pakistani Foreign Minister Agha Shahi rejected US$ 400 million US aid package and contended that such an acceptance would detract from rather than enhance the country's security. According to M. Shahi, Pakistan had planned to base its foreign policy with close ties with Islamic and non-aligned nations. Mr Shahi denied that Pakistan helped insurgents who were fighting Kabul's Soviet backed war, while Pakistani Government said that it was quite possible to frontier. (New York Times, March 6, 1980)

Carter Administration's officials said that US had not been notified of Pakistan's decisions to reject the offer (*ibid*). Carter Administration suspended Carter's plan to seek congressional approval of US$ 400 million economic and military aid package for Pakistan; the decision stemmed from the inability of governments to agree upon the size and content of aid; Pakistan's reluctance to accept aid offer was believed to be linked in part to a fear that such a stance might jeopardise its status as a non-aligned country, and partly to the sensitivity to

Soviet charges that Afghan rebels were being trained in refugee camps in Pakistan. (New York Times, March 6, 1980)

Pakistan's interest was in US aid revived after Washington's explanation that the offer had not been made on all-ornothing basis; Ambassador Arthur W Hummel Junior informed Pakistani Foreign Office that US$ 200 million in economic assistance was not to be tied to Pakistan's acceptance of another US$ 200 million in military sales credits (New York Times, March 13, 1980).

Pakistan's new foreign policy initiatives were reportedly tied to expectations that Saudi Arabia will provide it with some US$ 2 billion annually over next five years in military and economic assistance. At same time, Pakistan had not categorically rejected US aid proposal of US$ 400 million aid package, even though it had scorned the amount as 'peanuts'; only firm promises of contributions reported so far had been from Japan which offered US$ 128 million and Britain which promised US$ 38 million. Pledges of support, however, while welcome, appeared insignificant when set alongside economic and security problems facing Pakistan because of the crisis in Afghanistan and Iran. (New York Times, March 22, 1980)

Poul Harting, UN High Commissioner for Refugees, had been pressing US a for contributions to his commission's US $500 million budget to aid Afghan refugees in Pakistan (hi). (New York Times, March 15, 1981).

While Reagan Administration, tentatively decided and offered to Pakistan to get some US$ 580 in military and economic assistance for the next fiscal years; figure was more than double amount offered by Carter Administration and rejected by Pakistan as insufficient; there was some uncertainty about whether Pakistan would accept the aid and wanted to avoid giving Moscow pretext for intervention along Pakistan's border with Afghanistan. (New York Times, March 24, 1981)

Indian Prime Minister Indira Gandhi expressed her concern over the supply of arms sales to Pakistan (New York Times, July 28, 1980). US reported on renewed and extensive arms sales to Pakistan because of that country's importance to security of Persian Gulf and its situation as the only available conduit for supplying weapons to anti-Soviet guerrillas in Afghanistan (New York Times, March 5, 1981).

Reagan Administration's officials said that US might resume military training for Pakistan's armed forces (New York Times, March 25, 1981).

Indian Prime Minister Mrs Gandhi warned the US Government that military aid to Pakistan in the name of Afghanistan would be used against India (New York Times, April 10, 1981).

Diplomatic source reported that there were wide gaps between basic perceptions of Prime Minister Gandhi of India and Thatcher of England on the issue of US plan to renew arms deliveries to Pakistan; Thatcher approved the plan, but Gandhi feared that it would set back cause of peace in the area (New York Times, April 16, 1981).

In Indian Parliament, British Prime Minister Margaret Thatcher defended Pakistan's right to buy Western arms during a speech to Indian Parliament (New York Times, April 18, 1981).

Foreign Minister Agha Shahi reported on Reagan Administration's offer to his country for five year-economic and military assistance package, Pakistan was to get US$ 500 million in first year, but Secretary Haig indicated that there was nothing firm as to possible aid figure (New York Times, April 22, 1981).

US House Foreign Affairs Committee voted unanimously to defer action on lifting restrictions on military aid to Pakistan until State Department gives details of its aid requested and outlined a nuclear non-proliferation policy (New York Times, May 13, 1981).

Senate's Foreign Relations Committee voted to lift restrictions on aid to Pakistan and authorise US$ 100 million in economic in assistance in 82 (New York Times, May 15, 1981).

John B Oakes' article contended that US had planned to sell US$ 2 billion in arms to Pakistan which was an example of Reagan Administration's 'mindless militaristic substitute' for foreign or defence policy, this stance had already inflamed India which promoted peace and freedom for US and rest of the world (New York Times, July 8, 1981).

Reagan Administration planned to sell to Pakistan 15 F-16 fighter planes as part of its five-year economic and military assistance package (New York Times, June 13, 1981).

Foreign Minister Agha Shahi and US Under Secretary of State, James L. Buckley held talks in Islamabad, Buckley and Shahi discussed plans of US$ 2 billion in US economic and military aid (New York Times, June 14, 1981).

State Department announced US$ 3 billion aid programme for Pakistan; according to announcement on economic and military assistance it would bolster Pakistani defence against serious threat from Soviet troops in Afghanistan (New York Times, June 16, 1981).

Reagan Administration urged the Turkish Government to stop their secret shipment to Pakistan of million dollars worth of sensitive equipment that could be used to build atomic bomb. (New York Times, June 28, 1981).

Prime Minister Mrs Gandhi said that India would need to acquire sophisticated aircraft to match F-16 fighter bombers and was under way to purchase French made Mirage 2000's from France (New York Times, July 11, 1981).

Soviet Foreign Minister Gromyko, in an article published in New Delhi, said that Moscow could not stay aloof from Reagan Administration's plans to provide arms to Pakistan (New York Times, July 30, 1981).

Chief US delegate to UN, Jeane J Kirkpatrick, in New Delhi said that Reagan Administration had not believed that contemplated arms sales to Pakistan posed any real threat to India (New York Times, August 25, 1981).

Kirkpatrick, responded to suggestion by President Zia that US might delay promised shipment of F-16 fighter planes, and asserted that the planes and other military and economic aid would be sent (New York Times, August 29, 1981).

Pakistani Government accepted six year-plan of US$ 3.2 billion military and economic package offered by US; the agreement came after Reagan Administration planned to speed delivery of F-16 fighter planes for Pakistan; this came alongside on the eve of House of Foreign Affairs Committee's hearing to consider Administration's arguments for ending ban on aid to Pakistan even though Pakistan had refused to rule out developing ability to explode nuclear devices (New York Times, September 16, 1981).

Under Secretary, James L Buckley said nuclear detonation could cost Pakistan US$ 3.2 billion aid package - testimony, House Foreign Committee; he said that President Zia assured him that Pakistan would not develop nuclear weapons but he refused to rule out the developing potential to explode peaceful nuclear device (New York Times, September 17, 1981).

Representative Charles B Rangel stated that the Reagan Administration had planned to give Pakistan US$ 3 billion in military and economic aid (New York Times, September 19, 1981).

Senator Alan Cranston reported that Pakistan had begun to use fuel produced in its nuclear reactor, a development that could complicate Reagan Administration's proposed US$ 3.2 billion aid programme to Pakistan (New York Times, September 26, 1981).

House adopted an amendment on foreign aid bill for authorising the resumption of American aid policy for Pakistan. This was based on the concern regarding Pakistani nuclear programme; the policy measures provided for the prompt cut off of aid if Pakistan were to develop or acquire atomic weapons (New York Times, September 26, 1981).

Indian Prime Minister Indira Gandhi, in his speech at *the Commonwealth of Nations* meeting in Melbourne, Australia, while apparently speaking of prospects of US arms sales to Pakistan, condemned 'intrusion of outside interests' into regions of tension in which diplomatic endeavours had been making progress in easing strains (New York Times, October 1, 1981).

President Zia defended move to buy F-16 planes from US contending fighter planes were essential for country's defence (New York Times, October 18, 1981).

India planned to buy jet planes from France to counter US decision to supply Pakistan with 40 planes (New York Times, October 21, 1981).

President Zia welcomed US Congress's stance of passing a deadline to block jet sales (New York Times, November 25, 1981).

Indian Prime Minister Indira Gandhi expressed concern about US plans to sell F-16 fighters to Pakistan (New York Times, July 31, 1982).

Defence Department officials said that Pakistan refused to accept delivery of six F-16 jet fighter - bombers from US because they lack most advanced American electronic warfare systems; US Embassy official in Islamabad said that this dispute was on its way to being settled (New York Times, November 30, 1982).

President Zia said that he had achieved more than expected during his recent visit to Washington, including US commitment to continue military and economic aid (New York Times, January 1, 1981).

Vice President George Bush ended his four day visit to India. He defended US's arms sales to Pakistan's military Government, in reaction to Prime Minister Indira Gandhi's concern over the issue (New York Times, May 16, 1984).

Reagan Administration said that Pakistan had raised the possibility of buying American airborne early warning system to help defend its borders against raids by aircraft based in Afghanistan; he said that if Pakistan interested thus, then they could source Grumman E-2C all-weather planes (New York Times, October 12, 1984).

Senator, Claiborne Pell, in his report to Senates of Foreign Relations committee, warned that any major American arms sale to Pakistan would undermine prospects for improved relations between US and India (New York Times, December 23, 1984).

Reagan Administration proposed to send 100 portable anti-aircraft missiles and new air-to-air missiles to Pakistan to help it defend against increasing air incursions from Afghanistan flown by either Soviet or Afghan pilots. Many in Congress were worried about this sale of portable missiles, known as Stingers, since they were regarded as ideal weapons for terrorists who sought to strike down airliners (New York Times, July 12, 1985).

Defence Department approved more than US$ 200 million in arms sales to Pakistan (New York Times, September 10, 1985).

President Reagan had assured Pakistan despite American concern over continuation of aid, that Pakistan might be involved in smuggling nuclear weapons material from United States (New York Times, January 16, 1981).

In 1977, following India's nuclear test three years earlier, Senators John Glenn and Stuart Symington sought to prevent Pakistan from importing uranium-enrichment or nuclear fuel processing technology without international safeguards. If any country involved in such imports with Pakistan, sanctions against that country would be triggered. Building on this "stick", Secretary of State Henry Kissinger also added a "carrot" - a substantial conventional arms package if Pakistan agreed to forgo a plutonium reprocessing plant. The US proposal, while substantial, was seen by Pakistan in the light of 1965 and 1971. Only a nuclear device, not an uncertain US alliance, could protect Pakistan from India. While the United States was trying to persuade Pakistan away from fissile material production, Pakistan was redoubling its efforts and had wooed A. Q. Khan back from his work in Europe. The sanctions were a nuisance that could be overcome by presidential waiver during the Afghan war years. (*ibid*).

The government was unstable, however, and the Soviets invaded Afghanistan in 1979. For the first time in its history, Pakistan faced an extra regional threat at its doorstep. The US alliance, designed for such a contingency, finally came through, and massive amounts of US aid and equipment were moved into Pakistan to face off the Soviet threat. Pakistan could not defend itself from the Soviet forces conventionally, let alone defeat them. It decided, however, that working with the United States to support guerrillas in Afghanistan so as to take up the fight against the Soviets asymmetrically.

Pakistan, the United States and Saudi Arabia poured money into Islamic groups to fight the anti-Soviet jihad. While Pakistan and the United States were locked in proxy conflict with the Soviets over Afghanistan, Pakistan was an invaluable ally. Despite Islamabad's progress in pursuing nuclear devices, US economic and military aid continued to flow to support the anti-Soviet campaign. US dissuasive policy against nuclear development was designed around the belief that a conventionally wellarmed Pakistan would not pursue the nuclear track aggressively. (*ibid*)

CIA-ISI Collaborations

Pakistan's foreign policy stance shifted significantly in 1953 when it accepted the United State's offer of military and economic assistance in return for membership in an alliance system designed to contain international communism. When the administration of Dwight D. Eisenhower sought a series of alliances in the "Northern Tier", Pakistan, Iran, and Turkey,and in East Asia, Pakistan became a candidate for membership in each. In 1954, Pakistan signed a Mutual Defence Agreement with the United States and became a member of the Southeast Asia Treaty Organisation (SEATO). The following year, Pakistan joined Iran, Iraq and Turkey in the Baghdad Pact, later converted into the Central Treaty Organisation (CENTO) after Iraq's withdrawal in 1959. Pakistan also leased bases to the United States for intelligence gathering and communications facilities. Pakistan saw these agreements not as bulwarks against Soviet or Chinese aggression, but as a means to bolster itself against India. (http://www.fas.org/irp/world/pakistan/background.htm)

The CIA, in collaboration with the ISI of Pakistan, worked out the blueprint for the Afghan jihad. For the actual conduct of the war, the CIA acquired weapons and specialists in guerrilla warfare from different countries and delivered them, along with intelligence and surveillance information on Afghanistan, to the ISI. The ISI was responsible for transport of weapons to the border, supervising the training of Afghan fighters inside Pakistan, and coordination of their operations inside Afghanistan. While ISI was the main regional proxy in the operation, the second line included the intelligence services of Saudi Arabia and Egypt. Intelligence services of Britain, China, the Philippines, and even Israel were also involved. The basic lessons of Indo-China, Southern Africa, and Central America were applied with great care: this was to be an operation in which the CIA would be at more than arm's length. It would be a proxy war run through third and fourth parties.

As different tasks were subcontracted to different agencies, the blueprint of the war unfolded in a classified fashion. The point was to ensure the direct involvement of as few Americans as possible; fewer still were in direct contact with the Mujahedeen or their field commanders. While subcontracting removed American presence from the ground, and thus reducing the possibility of any direct damage to American personnel, its unintended consequence was to give substantial freedom to the subcontractors to bypass central command and deal directly with agencies such as the CIA or DEA. The result was a lack of coherence in overall American policy. (http//www.ciaisi\CIA and Reagan.htm).

The USA established CIA which subcontracted the anti-Soviet jihad through ISI. Pakistani intelligence being a division of the Pakistani army was not organised as a civilian intelligence service. ISI has been generally commanded by a two-star general, and its cadres have been drawn from the officer corps of the Pakistan army. They are organised in clandestine regional bureaus. The Afghan Bureau became the instrument of the anti-Soviet jihad. These were often Pashtuns, who had language and local identity and were seconded to the Bureau for long periods of time. Here a question arises that as to why did the CIA turn over its political programme through jihad to ISI. The CIA was scarred by its experience in Vietnam, and there was a sense of no more "hearts and minds" for USA. USA decided to let the Pakistanis figure out as to who were the winners and losers politically. USA decided that if Pakistan had a complicated regional agenda that was even more Islamist than US would like, so be it. US decided to focus on the main adversary, the Soviet Union and not to try to tell the Pakistanis as to how to run politics in the region. In the late 1980s, the CIA had established a counter terrorist Centre, organised by region and by target. Over the years, they've had cells for almost every terrorist target that has menaced the US or its allies. The Islamabad station recruited a group of paid Afghan agents who had worked with the agency in the 1980s to find Kansi, and they moved around southern Afghanistan trying to get a fix on him. Kansi eventually was captured by a walk-in informer. (http//www. cia- isi\thesecratehistoryofCIA.htm)

During the presidency of Ronald Reagan, there was sustained cooperation between the CIA and Pakistan's Inter Services Intelligence (ISI), and neither party had much interest in a negotiated settlement. Both intelligence agencies came to share a dual objective: militarily - to provide maximum firepower to the Mujahedeen and, politically - to recruit the most radically anti-Communist Islamists to counter Soviet forces. The combined result was to flood the region not only with all kinds of weapons but also with the most radical Islamist recruits. They flocked to ISI-run training camps in Pakistan, where they were "ideologically charged with the spark of holy war and trained in guerrilla tactics, sabotage and bombings". The Islamist recruits came from all over the world, not only Muslim-majority countries such as Algeria, Saudi Arabia, Egypt, and Indonesia, but also such Muslim-minority countries as the United States and Britain. (http://www. cia- isi\CIA and Reagan.htm)

During the regime of General Zia-ul-Haq, CIA provided ISI a large quantity of espionage equipment along with training and other information. Initially Pakistani intelligence was trained along British lines, but subsequently CIA trained 200 ISI officers in improved intelligence methods. Throughout the years of Soviet occupation of Afghanistan, relations between the United States and Pakistan were best characterised by close cooperation. Still, United States policy-makers became increasingly concerned that Zia and his associates - most notably, General Akhtar Abdur Rahman, the then head of the Directorate for Inter-Services Intelligence appeared to give preferential treatment to the Islamic fundamentalists, especially Mujahedeen leader Gulbaddin Hikmatyar.(http://www.fas.org/irp/world/pakistan/background.htm)

In 1985, in the White House, President Ronald Reagan while introducing the media, to a group of Afghan men who were leaders of the Mujahedeen, said: "These gentlemen are the moral equivalents of America's founding fathers". This was the moment when America tried to exploit extreme versions of political Islam in the struggle against the Soviet Union. Reagan presidency, who claimed that the defeat of US-backed dictatorships in the Third World was evidence that the Soviet Union was "on a roll" and it was Reagan who demanded that all possible resources be committed to Marshall-Plan so as to "roll back" the Soviet Union, "by all means necessary". Afghanistan, more than any other location, was the high point of the Cold War.

The Iranian Revolution of 1979 had a profound influence on the conduct of the Afghan War. It led to a restructuring of relations between the United States and political Islam. Prior to it, America saw the world in rather simple terms: on one side was the Soviet Union and militant Third World nationalism, which America regarded as a Soviet tool; on the other side was political Islam, which America considered an unqualified ally in the struggle against the Soviet Union. Thus, the United States supported the Sarekat-i-Islam against Sukarno in Indonesia, the Jamaat-i-Islami against Zulfiqar Ali Bhutto in Pakistan, and the Society of Muslim Brothers against Nasser in Egypt. Secret American aid to opponents of the pro-Soviet regime in Kabul had begun before the Soviet army invaded Afghanistan. CIA and State Department documents seized during the embassy takeover in Tehran reveal that the United States had begun quietly meeting Afghan-rebel representatives in Pakistan in April 1979, eight months before Soviet military intervention. This was confirmed by Zbigniew Brzezinski, President Carter's national security advisor, in a later interview with the Parisbased Le Nouvel Observateur (January 15-21, 1998): The former director of the CIA, Robert Gates, stated in his memoirs [From the Shadows] that American intelligence services had began to aid the Mujahedeen in Afghanistan six months before the Soviet intervention. "In this period, you were the national security advisor of President Carter. You therefore played a role in this affair. Was that correct? Brzezinski: Yes". According to the official version of history, CIA aid to the Mujahedeen began during 1980, that is to say, after the Soviet army invaded Afghanistan, December 24, 1979. But the reality, secretly guarded until now, is completely otherwise: Indeed, it was July 3, 1979 that President Carter signed the first directive for secret aid to the opponents of the pro-Soviet regime in Kabul. And that very day, I wrote a note to the president in which I explained to him that in my opinion, this aid was going to induce a Soviet military intervention.

Foreign Policy of US from the Carter to the Reagan presidency also accelerated shifted from containment to rollback. In Afghanistan, as in Nicaragua, the Carter administration had preferred a two-track approach, combining the carrot and the stick, approving moderate levels of covert support for anti-Communist allies, whether governments or groups, alongside a search for a negotiated settlement. Containment, in this sense, was guided by the search for coexistence. In contrast, the Reagan administration had absolutely no interest in arriving at negotiated settlements. Rather than coexistence, the point of the Reagan policy was payback: everything must be done to turn the Afghan War into the Soviet Union's Vietnam. The single objective was to bleed the Soviet Union white. The CIA was determined that nothing comes in the way of the "real task" in Afghanistan: "killing Russians". Among the more influential "bleeders" in Washington was Reagan's assistant secretary of defence, Richard Perle.

If the Reagan administration was predisposed to groups with hard-line ideological opposition to the Soviet Union and no interest in a compromise settlement, successive Pakistani governments had a pathological distrust of Afghan nationalism. This became clear when his cousin and former prime minister, Mohammad Daud deposed the Afghan king, Zahir Shah, in a bloodless coup, in July 1973. Daud put together a republican alliance of sections of the military and a wing of the Communist Party named after its newspaper, Percham (banner). The new government took up the popular cause of Pashtunistan, which demanded a homeland for the Pashtun people. Not only were roughly half of Afghanistan's population ethnic Pashtuns, millions of Pashtuns also lived in Pakistan's North-West Frontier Province (NWFP), on the other side of an artificial border drawn by the British at the height of their colonial empire in India. Fearful of Afghan nationalism, Pakistani governments were open to supporting anti-nationalist forces in Afghanistan, and Zia-ul-Haq's was no exception.

The ideological opposition to nationalism, including to Daud's authoritarian version, came mainly from Communists and Islamists, mostly university students and professors who were strongly international in their outlook. Increasing popular opposition to Daud's rule led to a second military coup known as the Saur Revolution that brought both factions of the Communist Party, Percham and Khalq (also named after its newspaper), into government. With this revolution of April 17,

1978, Communist "internationalism" became officially respectable, and Islamist "internationalism" was labelled subversive. Moderate and extremist Islamist radicals fled Kabul University for refuge in Pakistan, where they were welcomed.

The 1978 Communist coup also created a decisive shift in US relations with Pakistan. The Carter administration had cut aid to Pakistan in 1977, a response to both its dismal human-rights record at home - dramatised by the army's judicial murder of an elected prime minister, Zulfiqar Ali Bhutto - and the global implications of its accelerated nuclear programme. The coup and the Soviet invasion of Afghanistan changed all this: "literally days after the Soviet invasion, Carter was on the telephone with Zia offering him hundreds of millions of dollars in economic and military aid in exchange for cooperation in helping rebels". Zia held out for more, and the Carter-Zia partnership remained lukewarm. The real warming came with the Reagan administration, which offered Pakistan "a huge, six-year economic and military aid package which elevated Pakistan to the third largest recipient of US foreign aid" - after Israel and Egypt. (http://www.cia-isi\CIA and Reagan.htm)

In Kashmir issue, Initially, the ISI had no role in the collection of internal political intelligence except in Pakistan-Occupied Kashmir (POK) and the Northern Areas (NA-Gilgit and Balutistan). Ayub Khan, suspecting the loyalty and objectivity of the Bengali police officers in the Subsidiary Intelligence Bureau (SIB) of the IB in Dacca, the capital of the then East Pakistan, entrusted the ISI with the responsibility of the collection of internal political intelligence in East Pakistan. Similarly, Z.A. Bhutto, when faced with a revolt by Balochi nationalists in Balochistan after the liberation of Bangladesh in 1971, suspected the loyalty of the Balochi police officers of the SIB in Quetta and made the military officers of the ISI responsible for internal intelligence in Balochistan. Zia-ul-Haq expanded the internal intelligence responsi-bilities of the ISI by making it responsible not only for the collection of intelligence about the activities of the Sindhi nationalist elements in Sindh and for monitoring the activities of Shia organisations all over the country after the success of the Iranian Revolution in 1979, but also for keeping surveillance on the leaders of the Pakistan People's Party (PPP) of Mrs Benazir Bhutto and its allies which had started the Movement for the Restoration of Democracy (MRD) in the early 1980s. The ISI's Internal Political Division had Shah Nawaz Bhutto, one of the two brothers of Mrs Benazir Bhutto, assassinated through poisoning in the French Riviera in the middle of 1985, in an attempt to intimidate her into not returning to Pakistan for directing the movement against Zia, but she refused to be intimidated and returned to Pakistan.

Even in the 1950s, Ayub Khan had created in the ISI a Covert Action Division for assisting the insurgents in India's North-East and its role was expanded in the late 1960s to assist the Sikh Home Rule Movement of London-based Charan Singh Panchi, which was subsequently transformed into the so-called Khalistan Movement, headed by Jagjit Singh Chauhan. A myriad of organisations operating amongst the members of the Sikh diaspora in Europe, the US and Canada joined the movement at the instigation with the assistance of the ISI.

During the Nixon Administration in the US, when Dr Henry Kissinger was the National Security Adviser, the intelligence community of the US and the ISI worked in tandem in guiding and assisting the so-called Khalistan movement in the Punjab. The visits of prominent Sikh Home Rule personalities to the US before the Bangladesh Liberation War in December, 1971, to counter Indian allegations of violations of the human rights of the Bengalis of East Pakistan through counterallegations of violations of the human rights of the Sikhs in Punjab, were jointly orchestrated by the ISI, the US intelligence and some officials of the US National Security Council (NSC) Secretariat, then headed by Kissinger.

This covert collaboration between the ISI and the US intelligence community was also directed at discrediting Mrs Indira Gandhi's international stature by spreading disinformation about alleged naval base facilities granted by her to the USSR in Vizag and the Andaman and Nicobar, the alleged attachment of KGB advisers to the then Lt. Gen. Sunderji during Operation

Bluestar in the Golden Temple in Amritsar in June, 1984, and so on. This collaboration petered out after her assassination in October,1984.

The Afghan war of the 1980s saw the development of the secret action capabilities of the ISI by the CIA. A number of officers from the ISI's Covert Action Division received training in the US and many covert action experts of the CIA were attached to the ISI to guide it in its operations against the Soviet troops by using the Afghan Mujahedeen, Islamic fundamentalists of Pakistan and Arab volunteers. The encouragement of opium cultivation and heroin production and smuggling was also an offshoot of this co-operation. The CIA, through the ISI, promoted the smuggling of heroin into Afghanistan in order to make the Soviet troops heroin addicts. Once the Soviet troops were withdrawn in 1988, these heroin smugglers started smuggling the drugs to the West, with the complicity of the ISI. The heroin dollars have largely contributed to preventing the Pakistani economy from collapsing and enabling the ISI to divert the jihadi hordes from Afghanistan to J & K after 1989 and keeping them well motivated and well-equipped.

Even before Pokhran I nuclear test of 1974 conducted by India, the ISI had set up a division for the clandestine procurement of military nuclear technology from abroad and, subsequently, for the clandestine purchase and shipment of missiles and missile technology from China and North Korea. This division, which was funded partly by donations from Saudi Arabia and Libya, partly by concealed allocations in Pakistan's State budget and partly by heroin dollars, was instrumental in helping Pakistan achieve a military nuclear and delivery capability despite its lack of adequate human resources with the required expertise. Thus, the ISI, which was originally started as essentially an agency for the collection of external intelligence, developed into an agency adept in covert actions and clandestine procurement of denied technologies as well. The IB (Intelligence Bureau), which was patterned after the IB of British India, used to be largely a police organisation, but the post of Director-General (DG), IB, was no longer tenable only by police officers as it was in the past. Serving and retired military officers started being appointed in increasing numbers to senior posts in the IB, including the post of DG.(http//www. cia-isi\Pakistan's Inter-Services Intelligence(ISI).htm).

ISI was fashioned by Pakistan to be the main instrument against India for its nefarious designs but in no time it developed into a formidable tool of extra-constitutional governance within Pakistan also. All the Chief Executive Officers of Pakistan from Ayub Khan onwards, in order to promote their own and their party's interests, exploited it. Zia-ul-Huq's introduction of sweeping strains of fundamentalism in Pakistan infected ISI also, which, over time, made it a solid pillar of international Islamic fundamentalism. Within Pakistan, ISI has been often referred to as the third Estate, sometimes getting promoted to the status of second Estate when it supplanted the entire bureaucratic establishment. Its advice remains an important constituent of the internal and external policies in Pakistan. It has made and demolished governments in Pakistan, working with the military brass. Zulfiqar Ali Bhutto had used it for crushing the Baluch struggle, earlier it had served as an instrument of repression against Bengali aspirations in East Pakistan. Within Pakistan, the role of ISI has been akin to Gestapo in Nazi Germany or NKVD in Stalin's USSR. But, its main focus since its inception has been India.

It was necessary to understand that the historical process of creating a Muslim homeland in the Indian subcontinent had a certain inevitability about it. The two great civilisations, Hindu and Muslim, co-existed uneasily with each other in the sub-continent. With creation of Pakistan, the rulers of that country did not think that a final solution had been crafted. For them, the agenda of partition can be fulfilled only when more Muslim areas are carved out in the sub-continent. For more than a half century the ISI has been operating to achieve such goals.

Naturally, it identified India's fault lines and started working on them. Various tribal groups in India's North East, after independence, had felt troubled over questions concerning their ethnic and geopolitical identity. ISI was quick to step in to stoke insurgencies in these areas by providing inspirations and weapons. In all disaffected movements of North East, Naga, Mizo, Meiiti, Bodo, Ulfa, NLFT etc., ISI's footprints were clearly visible. All its activities were in the nature of proxy wars. It is incorrect to think that Pakistan embarked on a proxy war against India for the first time in J&K in the late 1980s. Such tactics have been followed from 1956 when Ayub Khan directed the ISI to develop links with Phizo. Thereafter, sponsoring subversion became a standard policy. Soon it was to morph into promotion of terrorism. The Khalistan imbroglio also owed much to the machinations of ISI though it must be added that the ISI was never in total comfort with the Sikhs or believed that a war of liberation could be started in Punjab. The exercise was commenced with the intention of creating a holding ground in Punjab so that a free hand could be available in J&K. The Khalistan idea is dead today but there can be no doubt that ISI will try to revive it should the scenario in Punjab deteriorate. ISI has succeeded in the intelligence encirclement of India through linkages in Nepal and Bangladesh. Through them, its current efforts are directed towards developing fissure lines in several states like Assam, West Bengal, UP, Gujarat, Maharashtra, Andhra Pradesh, Karnataka etc. Through support to Madrasas education and Jehadi minded groups, it seeks to convert the nationalism of Indian Muslims into trans-Arab Islamism. The Saudi effort to disseminate Wahabism worldwide helps this effort. ISI funds a number of websites to carry forward such propaganda and indoctrination. Talibanisation of Bangladesh is proving to be a great asset for it.

The ISI's belief that Islamic fundamentalism has become a worldwide unstoppable phenomenon. Ironically, the kick-start came from the US when President Carter in 1979, authorised the CIA to disseminate Islamic fundamentalism in Central Asia to destabilise the Soviet Union. Later, when the US converted the push into a Jihadi war against the Soviets in Afghanistan, the ISI's collaboration was sought. It was quick to take a ringside seat in the operations and became the coordinator and distributor of war materials received from US, UK, China, Saudi Arabia, Egypt etc. for conducting the Jihad. The ISI forged a strategic friendship with Osama Bin Laden and his Al Qaeda. To them, Jihad in Afghanistan was not only for the purpose of expelling the Soviets from the country, but, more importantly, to strengthen a staunch Islamic base in Afghanistan. Not long after, Pakistani rulers and sections of civil society started identifying with Jihadist world programme of Al Qaeda. Such objectives conflict with the US aims of combating international terrorism and capping the growth of Islamic fundamentalism. Therefore, ISI now plays a double role. While the Pakistani rulers provide lip service to controlling international terrorism, ISI quietly supports resurgent Talibans in Afghanistan, provides shelters to hunted Islamists and remains a protector of Salafist Wahabism (http://www. cia-isi\ BOOK REVIEW Fulcrum of Evil ISI-CIA-Al Qaeda Nexus.htm).

Growing Role of Political Islam

The common view on an irrational hostility to Islam and Muslims - a views often expounded by evangelical ministers in their meg-churches. Both views are deeply flawed and limited. Islam is what the Koran and Sharia Law say it is-above all Islam is what Muslims have done for 1,400 years. Sadly, few seem interested in these rather obvious sources. However, there is one view that is almost never discussed in the American media-the political analysis as to how Islamic radicalism became such a world-wide phenomena in the last 25 years. In the light of the recent upsurge in Islamic fundamentalism, surely this is the question to ask. There can be no reasonable doubt that poverty, lack of education and employment and above all the support of Islamism by nervous Islamic governments, hoping to detract attention from them, has been instrumental in radicalizing young Muslims. This is only part of the explanation. American foreign policy has played its own part in this tragedy.

Muslims from all backgrounds, agreed on one thing-namely, that US policy seeks to keep Muslim nations weak, with particular venom reserved for Israel: they are both disingenuous and wrong. They are disingenuous because Islamism is itself a profoundly political force, with a historically-based ambition of its own to restore Islamic imperialism anywhere and everywhere. They are wrong because the US has almost single-handedly, but inadvertently, helped to establish radical Islam all over the Middle East and Asia. Radical Islam of the late twentieth century had no better friend than Washington. The US, obsessed with the Soviet Union during the Cold War and wanting to expand the interests of its own capitalist elite, pursued a foreign policy that was blind to and ignorant of the Islamist monster it was nurturing. That monster has now become an international hydra whose victims are not American policy-makers but ordinary Americans, British commuters on London's under-ground, Australian tourists in Bali and of course thousands of innocent Muslims seeking only a peaceful life.

The US began nurturing radical Islam as early as the 1930s when it supported the rule of the Wahhabi Saudi family over Arabia in exchange for oil concessions. The Saudi royal family became obscenely wealthy in exchange for permitting the entering of America's security arrangements. In exchange for American patronage, the Saudis ensured a reliable flow of cheap oil. But oil was not all that is being exported. Saudi Arabia is the world's largest exporter of Islam and young Muslim men devoted to unrelenting jihad against the infidel. Their theology is Wahhabi Islam, an uncompromising and aggressive form of Islam, bent on conversion and promoting hatred of non-Muslims. By allowing this, the Saudi government, whose power is increasingly tenuous, has so far insulated itself from direct confrontation with the Wahhabi establishment. The Saudis, while denying legal equality and freedom of religion to non-Muslims, arrogantly fund mosques and Islamic centres in the US and Europe. The Organisation of the Islamic Conference (OIC) and related charities, being beholden to Saudi money, are only too willing to carry out the Wahhabi agenda. One can only imagine and shudder in disbelief to think about a scenario where the world's Christian countries form a similar international organisation to spread Christianity.

It is remarkable that the US Government, usually so eager to berate uncooperative nations over civil rights, is silent when it comes to Saudi Arabia. Neither George Bush nor Tony Blair, both bornagain Christians who reportedly pray together, has ever addressed the rights of religious minorities in Saudi Arabia. Nor would London or Washington ever dare to directly blame the Saudi government for Saudi sponsorship of Islamic terrorism. Perhaps the billions of dollars in arms sales to the Saudis is simply too good a business to upset. (http://www.American Foreign Policy and International Islamism.htm). The picture is equally depressing in other parts of the world where the US Government has supported political Islam. One of the worst massacres of the twentieth century was the genocidal attack that began in 1975, by the Indonesian government against the tiny Christian minority in the former Portuguese colony of East Timor. In 1975, Indonesia, the worlds' largest Muslim nation was led by the vehemently anti-communist Suharto regime. This was good enough for the US, who supplied Suharto with weapons and training. Both President Ford and Henry Kissinger were directly involved in giving Indonesia the nod of approval to invade East Timor. What happened next was pure genocide. The US-trained Indonesian army butchered a third of the East Timorese people. The invasion was not a mere land grab but a war to erase the East Timorese Catholic Church and Portuguese cultural influence. Throughout the East Timor genocide the American media and both the Ford and Carter administrations stayed silent - a silence tantamount to supporting the massacres. For a greater account of Kissinger's role in the East Timor massacre, see Christopher Hitchens' book "*The Trial of Henry Kissinger*".

Pakistan is one of the most troubling of Washington's "allies". The British, just prior to their withdrawal, carved Pakistan out of NW India in 1947 to meet the demands of Indian Muslims for an Islamic state. Since that time, Pakistan has been dominated by an elite plutocracy, the army and the mullahs. Pakistan was adopted by the US during the cold war as a reliable anti-communist bastionafter all the Pakistani elites and mullahs hate socialism more than they hate the infidel west. For most of its life, Pakistan has been the recipient of US weapons and financial support. The two nations were at their closest during the Soviet invasion of Afghanistan and throughout the 1980s both the Pakistani army and the CIA trained and armed the Afghan resistance against the Soviets. After the expulsion of the Soviets in 1989, the close relationship between Pakistani military intelligence and the Afghan Taliban flourished. This close bond continues to this day, despite Pakistan's outward alliance with the US's war on terror. Like Saudi Arabia, Pakistan is an ostensible ally of America; however, it is also a breeding ground of Islamic terrorists.

The simple overview of some of the major countries where US foreign policy has aligned itself with the Islamist agenda. Unless American policy-makers realised the dangers of promoting the Islamist agenda, it is not only the US but the entire world that will pay the price. Many nations have already begun to pay that price. The US must realise that Islamism is a political force that is utterly at odds with every notion of humanist tradition, be it western or eastern (http://www.American Foreign Policy and International Islamism.htm). American Foreign Policy provided a unique setting for experiments in synthesising Islamic principle with the needs of a modern state. Although Pakistan's independence movement was articulated in Western terminology and centred on the right to national self-determination, it was also rooted in the Islamic concept of society and of what constitutes legitimate political authority for a Muslim. The basis of the ideal Muslim polity is the Sharia, the sacred law of Islam as embodied in the Quran. Efforts to apply Quranic law in a modern political context have had a direct impact on Pakistan's political history and have also complicated the nation's constitutional evolution (http://www.photius.com/countries/pakistan/government/pakistan_ government_role_ of_i slam.html).

The process of Islamisation that has taken place in Pakistan, especially in the Zia years, has raised considerable concern about criminal law. In February 1979, President Zia promulgated a new legal code for Pakistan based on Islamic law and established the Federal Shariat Court to hear appeals arising from the new code. The Federal Shariat Court also has extensive other powers. It lies within the discretion of the court of first instance to decide whether to try a case under civil or sharia law. If the latter, then the appeals process goes to the Federal Shariat Court, rather than to the High Courts. Sharia law was not intended to replace the criminal code but to bring specific parts of it in accordance with the Quran and the Sharia. It's most notable provisions are contained in the Hudood ordinances promulgated in 1979. The first ordinance deals with offenses against property, the second with zina (adultery) and zina-bil-jabr (rape), the third with qazf (false accusation of zina), and the fourth with prohibition of alcoholic beverages. Under the ordinances, there are two levels of cases: Hudood cases, which have particularly strict Islamic evidentiary requirements and call for specific "Islamic" punish-ments; and Tazir cases, where the evidence requirements are less strict and the punishments less draconian. A later decision by the Federal Shariat Court has made defiling the name of the Prophet Muhammad punishable by a mandatory death penalty. This decision has raised concerns in Pakistan's small Christian community and especially among the badly persecuted Ahmadiyya religious minority. Orthodox Pakistani Muslims consider Ahmadiyyas heretical, and the group has been prohibited from asserting any claim to being Muslim even the use of everyday Islamic greetings.As a headed crime, rape is punishable by hanging; adultery and fornication, as well as qazf, by stoning to death. Crimes against property of substantial value call for amputation of hands or feet. Public drunkenness and, in the case of Muslims, any consumption of alcohol, is punishable by flogging.

For the most part, Islamic punishments have not been carried out, the sole exception being flogging, which has been imposed primarily for Tazir crimes, as well as for narcotics-related crimes. In addition, alleged political crimes also resulted in flogging during the last period of martial law (1977- 85). Hudood sentences of amputation have been passed but either have been reversed on appeal or have not been carried out.

Occasional stoning for adultery have always taken place in tribal and other rural areas, but no sentence of stoning under the 1979 Hudood laws has been carried out.

The Federal Shariat Court has been involved mainly with non-criminal matters, aside from the review of Hudood convictions, which in most cases the Federal Shariat Court has reversed. In other matters, such as provision of equal treatment under the law and requirement for a standard of evidence, its application of Islamic principles has even served as a liberalising factor, including in the military justice system. Laws passed in the 1980s give the victim of a murder or other violence, or the victim's heirs, the right to inflict an equivalent harm. At the same time, however, there is a legal alternative in payment of blood money, which enables wealthy Pakistanis to avoid punishment by paying money. Under the law, only half of the amount must be paid if the victim is female. In 1984, parts of the Indian Evidence Act of 1872 were changed with much fanfare to meet Islamic criteria, but there was little substantial change. Demands by Islamic enthusiasts that the testimony of two women be considered the equivalent of that of one man were met only symbolically. The Hudood ordinances, however, do contain evidential provisions that discriminate sharply against women. (http://atheism.about.com/library/FAQs/islam/countries/bl_PakistanIslamPolitics.htm)

In Pakistan, moreover, the war on terror intersects perilously with the threat of weapons of mass destruction. Yet perhaps the greatest danger comes from Pakistan's own tendency towards selfdestruction- not from technology or the conflict with India, but rather from the domestic identity wars that are reaching a boiling point. The muddle in Pakistan has always been about its identity as a nation-state. Created by coalitions of Muslim politicians, feudals, industrialists, and Western educated civil servants who foresaw the likelihood of their community's decline in an undivided post-British India, this Muslim country has survived few of the tests of nationhood unscathed. In 1971, when the Muslims of East Pakistan won their bloody liberation from the Muslims of West Pakistan,

Pakistan became a rump state, and the idea of a Muslim homeland in the subcontinent should have been wrecked on the shoals of linguistic, ethnic, and geographic differences. But thirty-two years later, with more mullahs in government than ever before vociferously demanding that Pakistan be true to its Islamic statehood. Pakistanis are arguing once more about just how Islamic the Pakistani republic should be and who will control its fate. Was the slippery slope towards an uncompromising Islamism inevitable in a country created by Muslim liberals out of an argument that Indian Muslims constituted much more, culturally and politically, than a minority? Can the global Islamists today take advantage of the contradictions of Pakistan's birth to haunt the state or have Pakistanis built up enough history to claim a non-Islamist future for their country?

Only two years after the secession of East Pakistan, Pakistan's Constitution of 1973 reiterated its Islamic direction. It stated that sovereignty belongs to Allah alone and that "all existing laws shall be brought in conformity with the injunctions of Islam as laid down in the holy Quran and Sunnah". It was not until the 1980s, however, that constitutional text became political fact. Global circumstances facilitated the process of Islamisation, just as they are doing again today. The Iranian revolution created a new and religious atmosphere. The need for Pakistan to help fight the Soviets in Afghanistan in the 1980s was also a reason. It was not the mullahs, though, who successfully Islamised the country, and re-shaped the idea of Pakistan, in the 1980s. Adding to US concerns about Pakistan's domestic political developments are increasing signs of "Islamisation" and anti-American sentiment there. (CRS Report, February 14, 2005, p. 20) The Pakistani army, which was significantly radicalised by Gen. Zia's policies in the 1980s, continues to be home to Muslim hardliners at the middle and lower ranks. (*ibid*, p. 22)

The United States abetted Zia's domestic transformation, including the implementation of Islamic laws particularly painful for women, by financing him generously. The meagre opposition that Zia faced at home came largely from groups that were not of much interest to Bennett Jones and Weaver, who generally neglected the battles over ideas and cultures. It is especially egregious that they ignored Pakistan's women's movement, which has been widely emulated for its principles and its strategies. These remarkable women were among the first to challenge Zia's dictatorial and Islamisation policies, and to question openly the right of the mullahs to interpret Islam exclusively or to claim sole possession of the definition of Muslim identity. While the politicians largely sat silent on the sidelines, the women took to the streets to call for greater democracy in Pakistan. It is these women who, at a high cost to themselves, have been most articulate about the rights of minorities, the protection of women, the education of the illiterate in their rights under Islam, and more.

Zia's civilian successors did little to reverse his policies. The General opened up a political space for the mullahs that seems nearly impossible to close today. And in turn the mullahs today are opening up a political space for the militants. The Pakistan of Mohammed Ali Jinnah- Muslim but secular, and democratic, and a Muslim country practicing freedom of religion- has mostly been jettisoned. The great constitutional strategist for Muslim rights and citizenship now represents an antiquated secularism. In fact, "secularism" is a tarnished, even incendiary word in Pakistan, denoting ladiniyat or "irreligiosity". And, depending on the political tenor of the moment, Jinnah is alternatively reviled by the Islamists as a false Muslim or claimed as the truest believer in an Islamic state. To call Jinnah secular today is, as one leading Islamist intellectual puts it, to follow "the American vision".

But the Jamaat is Maududist, and therefore of enormous interest to anybody concerned with Islam and global politics. It was founded in 1941 by Maulana Abu'l Ala Maududi, who was arguably the most influential radical Islamist thinker of the twentieth century. Maududi's thought and the Jamaat's practice should place Pakistan at the intellectual epicentre of the wave of Islamist radicalism sweeping through the world today, and not, as often thought, as a secondary staging ground for Arab terror activities. It was Maududi's work, circulated in Egypt in 1951, that helped radicalise the now world-famous Sayyid Qutb, the pre-eminent intellectual patron of Arab jihadis. And it was from Maududi and Qutb that Ayatollah Khomeini drew some of his historical thinking and rhetorical force. The writings of Maududi, Qutb, and Hassan Al Banna of the Muslim Brotherhood inspired the Arab Mujahideen in the Afghan wars of the 1980s. Reading Qutb can feel a lot like re-reading Maududi, particularly in his assault on Westernised (that is to say, false) Muslims.

For an Islamic revolution, said Maududi, "the mind of man should first be disabused of the idea of independence and mankind should realise that the universe in which we live is governed by an All Powerful Sovereign. It behoves us to deny obedience to all authority which does not itself owe allegiance to Him and to refuse to serve any person or group of persons who act independently of the Will and Purpose of the Creator. This is the bedrock basis of all reformation". If democracy means human sovereignty or man-made laws, then Maududi had no use for it, and nor (despite their use of political partyhood and electoral campaigns) can his party, the Jamaat.

Maududi first opposed the creation of Pakistan, decrying the un-Muslimness of the pro-partition leadership. He lambasted those leaders whose minds were enslaved by Western education. He also denounced secular nationalism, which he called the "curse of the nation-state". The "distinguishing mark of an Islamic state", he said, "*is its complete freedom from all traces of nationalism*". In the new Pakistan, Maududi instructed his party's exclusive membership- a highly organised vanguard of moral men (and, later, moral women) to toil relentlessly for the creation of an Islamic state. The Jamaat transitioned easily from anti- Hinduism to nationalistic anti-Indianism.

Often jailed in Pakistan, Maududi had an uncomplicated, uncompromising, and exclusionary vision; a radical summons to the spiritual renovation of Muslims led astray by Western thought that falsely separated personal religion from political religion. Maududi's polemic was as internal to Islam as Qutb's. His book *Purdah and the Status of Women in Islam*, which appeared in 1939, has become a central Islamist text, endlessly reprinted and translated. It argues for sexual segregation as a fundamental requirement for ordering men's desire, and for limiting moral depravity, nudism, licentiousness, and all such Western diseases.

Foreign cultures were the most pernicious threat to Muslim societies, and so Maududi demanded a re-orientation of education policy that would give rise to a differently educated Muslim leadership. He discarded the narrow madrasa mentality of Islamist traditionalists, which eschewed sciences and technologies that might be gleaned from abroad, and also what he saw as the Westernised social sciences and the absence of religious studies in the curriculum of the modernists: "One of these fails to prepare people to shoulder the practical responsibilities of worldly life, while the other fails to provide any religious guidance or moral orientation. These conflicting systems of education have produced people with fundamentally different outlooks which has resulted in a dangerous internal conflict in Muslim society". In one sense, Maududi was right: Pakistan's current catacomb of educational systems- in English and in Urdu, in madrasas, in public schools, and in private schoolsis producing a highly compartmentalised citizenry with few shared values or skills.

Militant Islamists wield the most guns and exercise the most street power, but it is wrong to buy their argument that they have a superior claim to speak for Pakistanis because the country was constituted as a Muslim nation and is constitutionally an Islamic republic. Jinnah may not have won the Muslim entity he bargained for, but the critical fact is that there has always been a healthy-indeed, a precious- absence of agreement on what constitutes an Islamic state in Pakistan among jurists, theologians, and political leaders. (Even the MMA parties today disagree bitterly on theological principles and political goals) The majority of Pakistanis do not seem to want the mullahs to define their politics. These encouraging realities are precisely what have protected the Pakistani state from dissolving in a bloody war.

The decisive event for the army vis-á-vis India came earlier, in 1971, when the genocidal civil war that left up to three million dead resulted in the creation of Bangladesh; and in India's intervention in that war, and the subsequent humiliating surrender of ninety thousand prisoners of war. The army has never forgotten. The destruction of Pakistan in 1971 should have also put paid to the notion that the army was the saviour of the nation. Instead, less than a decade later, Zia's dictatorship sought salvation for Pakistan in an Islamised army. He promoted the deliberate Islamisation of the middle and lower ranks of the army (many members of which are now higher-ups) and the gradual militarisation of the madrasas. In the decade that followed, as Pakistan was cut off economically and militarily from interactions with America in particular, the introversion and the anti-Americanism of the junior officers increased. As Weaver reports, Musharraf had remarked to General Anthony Zinni that his biggest problem arises from the fact that "seventy-five per cent of my officers have never been out of Pakistan".

Zia's legacy contrasts sharply with the social liberalism of one of his predecessors, General Ayub Khan; which was embodied in the Muslim Family Laws Ordinance of 1962, the most liberal body of family law known to Pakistan. And Zia's Islamisation programmes may have rendered both Ayub's socially liberal achievements in family law as well as Musharraf's present ambitions beside the point. Whether or not Musharraf truly wants to fashion "a modernist, liberal" Pakistan, as Bennett Jones believes, there is very little scope for him now to win the ideological war for Pakistan, at least incrementally. Fighting Zia's legacy would require taking a page from Zia's book - using the full force of his vision to shape a new beginning.

The Kashmir conflict has been promoted by successive Pakistani leaders, civilian and military, to reinforce Pakistani nationalism whenever it has been politically expedient. The Pakistani argument for Kashmir has merit; but whatever the historical rights and wrongs of the issue, continuing the wars in Kashmir in order to "bleed India", where an estimated thirty to sixty thousand people have died, has given Pakistan's leaders not a progressive nationalism, but a way to gain populist support, an expensive hostility, and a militarised society. The Pakistan of the army, followed closely by the Pakistan of the civilian politicians, has long put the freedom of Kashmiris from Indian rule ahead of the freedom of Pakistanis from illiteracy, inequality, and poverty.

Besides, there is also the "cement" of anti-Americanism, which is growing among Pakistanis. The religious parties raise a daily cacophony of threats to America-that infiltrator of secularism and "the colours of Western thought and civilisation", says a Jamaat leader. Islamist terrorists kill Americans in Pakistan. Millions of other Pakistanis feel trapped between these Islamists and what they view as a dominant and un-self-questioning America (http://wwwpskistsn's islamisation.htm).

References

Ayoob, Mohammed (1985), "Dateline Pakistan: A Passage to Anarchy?" *Foreign Policy,* Summer-1985.

Chopra, V.D. (1985), *Pentagon Shadow over India."* Patriot pub.

Foreign Policy, Spring-1986, pp. 148-166.

Frankel, Francine R. (1986), "Play the India Card," *Foreign Policy,* Spring-1986.

Harrison, Selig (1986), "Cut a Regional Deal," *Foreign Policy,* Spring-1986.

http//www. cia-isi\CIA and Reagan.htm

http//www. cia-isi\CIA and Reagan.htm

http//www. cia-isi\Pakistan's Inter-Services Intelligence(ISI).htm

http//www. cia-isi\Pakistan's Inter-Services Intelligence(ISI).htm

http//www. cia-isi\the secrate history of CIA.htm

http//www.cia-isi\thesecratehistoryofCIA.htm

http://www. cia-isi\ BOOK REVIEW Fulcrum of Evil ISI-CIA-Al Qaeda Nexus.htm

http://www. cia-isi\ BOOK REVIEW Fulcrum of Evil ISI-CIA-Al Qaeda Nexus.htm

http://www. cia-isi\CIA and Reagan.htm

http://www. cia-isi\CIA and Reagan.htm

http://www. Strategic Insights , Dissuasion and Regional Allies - The C.htm

http://www. Strategic Insights , Dissuasion and Regional Allies - The C.htm

http://www. zia-reagan 1.htm

http://www. zia-reagan 1.htm

http://www. zia-reagan 2.htm

http://www. zia-reagan 2.htm

http://www.American Foreign Policy and International Islamism.htm/ American Foreign Policy and International Islamism

http://www.American Foreign Policy and International Islamism.htm) American Foreign Policy and International Islamism

http://www.American Foreign Policy and International Islamism.htm

http://www.American Foreign Policy and International Islamism.htm

http://www.country-data.com/cgi-bin/query/r-9826.html

http://www.country-data.com/cgi-bin/query/r-9826.html

http://www.country-data.com/cgi-bin/query/r-9826.html

http://www.country-data.com/cgi-bin/query/r-9826.html

http://www.country-data.com/cgi-bin/query/r-9850.html

http://www.country-data.com/cgi-bin/query/r-9901.html

http://www.country-data.com/cgi-bin/query/r-9901.html

http://www.country-data.com/cgi-bin/query/r-9901.html

http://www.country-data.com/cgi-bin/query/r-9901.html)

http://www.country-data.com/cgi-bin/query/r-9922.html

http://www.country-data.com/cgi-bin/query/r-9922.html) http://atheism.about.com/library/FAQs/islam/countries/bl_PakistanIslamPolitics.htm

http://www.fact Sheet United States and Pakistan Long-Term Strategic Partners.htm).

http://www.fact Sheet United States and Pakistan Long-Term Strategic Partners.htm

http://www.faithfreedom.org/oped/PaoloBassi51017.htm

http://www.faithfreedom.org/oped/PaoloBassi51017.htm

http://www.fas.org/irp/world/pakistan/background.htm

http://www.fas.org/irp/world/pakistan/background.htm

http://www.fas.org/irp/world/pakistan/background.htm

http://www.fas.org/irp/world/pakistan/background.htm

http://www.Pakistan Facilities.htm

http://www.Pakistan Facilities.htm).

http://www.photius.com/countries/pakistan/government/pakistan_government_rol e_of_islam.html

http://wwwpskistsn,s islamisation.htm.

http://wwwpskistsn's islamisation.htm.) Mahnaz Ispahani, Former Council Adjunct Senior Fellow for South and West Asia.....http://www.cfr.org/publication.html?id=6052

Karp, Craig M. (1986), "The War in Afghanistan," *Foreign Affairs*, Summer-1986.

Kissinger, Henry (1979), *White House Years*, Boston: Little, Brown and Company.

Kronstadt, K. Alan (2005), "Pakistan's Domestic Political Developments", *CRS Report for Congress*, Foreign Affairs, Defense, and Trade Division. Updated February 14, 2005.

Kux, Dennis (2001), *The United States and Pakistan, 1947-2000: Disenchanted Allies,* Washington, D.C.: Woodrow Wilson Center Press.

Laber, Jeri, "*A Dilemma For Pakistan*," New York Times, October 17, 1986.

Leo, E. Rose and Noor A. Hussain (1987), United State and Pakistan forum: Relations with the major powers, Lahaur.

LePoer, Barbara Leitch (2001), "Pakistan-U.S. Relations" , *CRS* Issue Brief for Congress Received through the CRS Web, Order Code IB94041, Foreign Affairs, Defense, and Trade Division. Updated March 15, 2001.

McMahon, Robert J. (1994), "The Cold War On The Periphery: The United States, India Pakistan," Columbia University Press, New York, 1994

(New York Times, January 1, 1980)

(New York Times, January 8, 1980)

(New York Times, January 18, 1980)

(New York Times, January 19, 1980)

(New York Times, January 22, 1980)

(New York Times, January 25, 1980)

(New York Times, January 29, 1980)

(New York Times, February 1, 1980)

(New York Times, February 1, 1980)

(New York Times, March 6, 1980)

(New York Times, March 6, 1980)

(New York Times, March 13, 1980)
(New York Times, March 22, 1980)
(New York Times, March 15, 1981)
(New York Times, March 24, 1981)
(New York Times, April 22, 1981)
(New York Times, July 28, 1980)
(New York Times, March 5, 1981)
(New York Times, March 15, 1981)
(New York Times, March 24, 1981)
(New York Times, March 25, 1981
(New York Times, April 10, 1981)
(New York Times, April 16, 1981)
(New York Times, April 18, 1981)
(New York Times, April 22, 1981)
(New York Times, May 13, 1981)
(New York Times, May 15, 1981)
(New York Times, July 8, 1981)
(New York Times, June 13, 1981)
(New York Times, June 14, 1981)
(New York Times, June 16, 1981)
(New York Times, June 28, 1981)
(New York Times, July 11, 1981)
(New York Times, July 30, 1981)
(New York Times, August 25, 1981)
(New York Times, August 29, 1981)
(New York Times, September 16, 1981)
(New York Times, September 17, 1981)
(New York Times, September 19, 1981)
(New York Times, September 26, 1981)
(New York Times, September 26, 1981)
(New York Times, October 1, 1981)
(New York Times, October 18, 1981)
(New York Times, October 21, 1981)
(New York Times, November 25, 1981)
(New York Times, July 31, 1982)
(New York Times, November 30, 1982)
(New York Times, January 1, 1981)

(New York Times, May 16, 1984)

(New York Times, October 12, 1984)

(New York Times, December 23, 1984)

((New York Times, July 12, 1985)

(New York Times, January 16, 1981)

((New York Times, September 10, 1985)

New York Times, October 17

New York Times, October 30, 1986

Newsweek, July 7, 1986, pp. 33-35.

Nye Jr. Joseph S. (1986), "Pakistan's Bomb Could Kill Us All", *Washington Post*, November 9, 1986.

Reiss, Spencer (1986), "Bhutto's Test of Wills," *Newsweek*, August 25, 1986.

Tahir-Kheli, Shirin (1982), The United States and Pakistan: The Evolution of an Influence Relationship, New York: Praeger.

Van Hollen, Christopher (1980), "Leaning on Pakistan, *Foreign Policy*, Spring -1980.

Venkatramni, M.S. (1982), *American Role in Pakistan, 1947-1958*, New Delhi: Radiant Publications.

Washington Post, November 9, 1986.

Watson, Russell and Donna Foote (1986), "Avenging Angel," *Newsweek*, July 7, 1986.

Weisman, Steven R.(1986), "Civilian Areas Raided By Russians, Pakistanis Say," *New York Times*, October 30, 1986.

Ziring, Lawrence (1983), "The United States and Pakistan: Troubled Alliance," *Journal of South Asian and Middle Eastern Studies*, Summer-1983.

Ziring, Lawrence (1983), Journal of South Asian and Middle Eastern Studies, Summer-1983.

Chapter 4

Ignoring Nuclear Proliferation

One crucial importance of President Ronald Reagan's Pakistan policy that could never be ignored was Pakistan's successful quest for a nuclear weapon capability. For a number of reasons, US non-proliferation legislation and the administration's diplomatic efforts tended to focus primarily on Pakistan, rather than India or China, the latter of which is already recognised as a legitimate nuclear weapon state under the NPT.1. The lack of "symmetry" in the treatment of India and Pakistan that is now being criticised by Pakistan and some in Congress was never a deliberate policy decision, however. Rather, US non-proliferation policies towards both countries arose out of special historical.

Nuclear proliferation is a term now that is used to describe the spread of nuclear weapons, fissile material, and weapons-applicable nuclear technology and information. There are nations which are not recognised as "nuclear weapon States" by the *Treaty on the Non-proliferation of Nuclear Weapons*, also known as the Nuclear Non-proliferation Treaty or NPT. Nuclear non-proliferation Treaty came in light just after the World War II, when the Truman Administration proposed the Baruch Plan of 1946, named after Bernard Baruch, America's first representative to the United Nations Atomic Energy Commission. The Baruch Plan1, which drew heavily from the Acheson-Lilienthal Report of 1946, proposed the verifiable dismantlement and destruction of the US nuclear arsenal (which, at that time, was the only nuclear arsenal in the world) after all governments had cooperated successfully to accomplish two things: (1) the establishment of an "international atomic development authority", which would actually own and control all military-applicable nuclear materials and activities, and (2) the creation of a system of automatic sanctions, which not even the UN Security Council could veto, and which would proportionately punish states attempting to acquire the capability to make nuclear weapons or fissile material. Although the Baruch Plan enjoyed wide international support, it failed to emerge from the UNAEC because the Soviet Union planned to veto it in the Security Council. Still, it remained official American policy until 1953, when President Eisenhower made his "Atoms for Peace" proposal before the UN General Assembly. Eisenhower's proposal led eventually to the creation of the International Atomic Energy Agency (IAEA) in 1957. Under the "Atoms for Peace" programme thousands of scientists from around the world were educated in nuclear science and then were dispatched home, where many later pursued secret weapons programmes in their home country. Efforts to conclude an international agreement to limit the spread of nuclear weapons did not begin until the early 1960s, after four nations (i.e., the US, Soviet Union, Britain and France) had acquired nuclear weapons (see List of countries with nuclear weapons for more information). Although these efforts stalled in the early 1960s, they renewed once again in 1964, after the People's Republic of China detonated a nuclear weapon and became the fifth nation to have acquired nuclear weapons. In 1968, govern-ments represented at the Eighteen Nation Disarmament Committee (ENDC) finished negotiations on the text of the NPT. In June 1968, the UN General Assembly endorsed the NPT with General Assembly Resolution 2373 (XXII), and in July 1968, the NPT opened for signature in Washington, DC, London and Moscow. The NPT entered into force in March 1970.

Among other things, US non-proliferation legislation has focused on the *transfer* of nuclear materials and technology, not their indigenous development. It is widely acknowledged that this approach was adopted in part to avoid having Israel fall under the scope of non-proliferation-based aid restrictions. Coincidentally, this also benefited India, which like Israel has an indigenous capability for developing nuclear weapons.

The United States has not ignored India's nuclear activities, however. India's 1974 nuclear test served as a major spur to the passage of the Nuclear Non-Proliferation Act of 1978. As a result of the passage of that legislation, the United States eventually abrogated a 1963 nuclear cooperation agreement that otherwise committed it for 30 years to make commercial sales of enriched uranium for India's US-built nuclear power station at Tarapur, near Bombay, due to India's refusal to put all of its nuclear facilities under international inspection. However, India had already tested a nuclear device before the adoption of the sections of the foreign assistance act that sought to check Pakistan's drive to acquire nuclear weapons.

Security is basically a relational phenomenon and an ambiguous concept. (Wolfers, 1962, p. 10). It is a broader idea than power, and it has the useful feature of incorporating much of the insight, which derives from the analysis of power (Buzan, http://jpr.sagepub.com/cgi/content/refs/21/2/109).

In his theory of international politics, Kenneth Waltz identified that states can balance against threats. States can balance externally, through alliances, or internally, through military preparations (Waltz, 1979, p. 168). Both types of balancing incur costs, alliances bring commitments and the threat of unwanted entanglement, while military preparations divert scarce resources from other important projects. In the modern world, states operate in a "self-defence" system in which threats to national security are omnipresent. Most of the 'weak' and 'small' states, in particular, have difficulties meeting challenges from powerful neighbours, since such states are by definition limited in their ability to build sizeable and well-equipped military machines (Handel, 1981, pp. 56-76).

In other words, strong states with mature institutions, well-defined territories and strong national identities may well promote the security of their people and be able to counter any external threat (Sorensen, *Security Dialogue*, p. 377). In contemporary times, the ultimate balance is nuclear weapons. States can either seek nuclear guarantees from established nuclear powers, or they can construct their own nuclear weapons. In this regard, Michael Handel analyses the place of weak states in the international system, claiming that a few small states reconcile themselves to "defensive nihilism", the abandonment of hope to establish an effective defence (Handel, 1981, p. 77). Waltz believes that "the gradual spread of nuclear weapons will promote peace and reinforce international stability because nuclear weapons induce caution between adversaries who possess them" (Waltz, 1981, p. 30). Nuclear weapons are incomparably more devastating than conventional military power. They reduce the probability of a major global war because nuclear weapons can be suicidal. Moreover, nuclear weapons can make it possible to compress the fury of war without the collapse of the state. They can change the speed, control the sequence of events and can provide protection from the threat of military defeat and total destruction (Thayer, *'Security Studies,* 1995, pp. 150-155). Hans Morgenthau has observed that nuclear weapons can reduce the conventional threats posed by adversaries and increase states security in an anarchic world (Morgenthau, *American Political Science Review*, 1964, p. 35).

The two Third World countries which are traditional enemies, and in close proximity. Their mutual disputes and conflicts are endemic and quickly come to engage critical interests. One strategist contends, "Leaders of the Third World may be ready to risk nuclear confrontation, irrespective of high levels of nuclear damage, in pursuit of their national interest or objectives" (Kaiser, 1989, pp. 123-136). Of most concern is the fear that inter-state conflict in Third World states can also socialise states so that they consider military force, even nuclear weapons, in terms of waging war, rather than in terms of deterrence. It seems equally clear that defensively minded states cannot compete against powerful states and only nuclear weapons can provide a strong guarantee that a state would not be put in a position of losing everything, even at the hands of an aggressor, which also has nuclear weapons.

The birth of Pakistan's nuclear programme was in direct response to its defeat in the Bangladesh War in 1971 and after India's nuclear test in 1974. These two events provided Pakistan with evidence of its insecurity in regard to both its sovereignty and its inability to deter possible Indian aggression. Nuclear weapons were seen in Pakistan's power corridors as an "equalizer", making up for Pakistan's lack of strategic depth and conventional asymmetry. Pakistan's development of the nuclear option is the result, at least in part, of its lack of success in its competition with India (Hoyt, 2005, pp. 113-115). Accordingly, nuclear weapons have always formed the centre piece in Pakistan's search for "strategic equality" with India, which has deep historical roots stretching back to the partition of the two countries in 1947.

Pakistan's nuclear preparation and doctrine have been based on fairly clear and straightforward means to forge a credible deterrent to counter India. In pursuit of this aim, Pakistan has been forced to shift from a policy of external balancing to one of internal balancing. Throughout its history, Pakistan's foreign policy has been dominated by the determination to incorporate Kashmir into the republic; its security policy, in turn, has been formed by the perceived threat from India, defined in terms of Kashmir and the integration of the Pakistani state. Since 1970s, Pakistan has been engaged in a major nuclear programme to enhance its nuclear weapons capability as a deterrent against India's overwhelming conventional and nuclear superiority. Thus, strategically, Pakistan's nuclear programme is driven mainly by its perception of threat and security concerns about India, which it claims has not fully accepted the existence of Pakistan as an independent country. Pakistan has always been a weak and vulnerable country and it would face great difficulty in prevailing in a war against Indian resources as its own, both military and civilian, are too limited. Pakistan cannot expect to match India tank for tank or gun for gun because the numbers are too great.

According to William Pfaff, India's intransigence on bilateral disputes and her nuclear superiority have made Pakistani leaders feel compelled to see nuclear weapons as a hedge, in order to stay in the game (Pfaff, International Herald Tribune, 3 June 1998).

Pakistan launched its own nuclear weapons programme and continued to expand its ability to produce weapons-grade nuclear material without adherence to International Atomic Energy Agency (IAEA) safeguards and continued to resort to clandestine nuclear trade to advance its nuclear programme. The Pakistani military and political elite as an important component in national power always regarded technology, and in its nuclear weapons it has always aspired to a high-tech edge over its rivals. As a result, the Pakistani high regard for smart weapons and technologically advanced support systems has intensified. Prime Minister Zulfikar Ali Bhutto once declared that "Pakistanis would rather eat grass or leaves, or even go hungry, but we will get one of our own, than surrender the nuclear option" (Chellaney, *Survival*, Vol. 35, No. 3, autumn 1993, p. 122). Pakistan's nuclear policy was founded in the 1950s and the US "Atomic for Peace" programme trained Pakistani scientists in nuclear-reactor technology. They also enabled Pakistan to buy a 5 MW swimming pool type research reactor and fuel, too small to have any military significance, which became fully operational in 1965; it has been used mainly for training purposes. A Canadian 137 MW heavy-water type power plant reactor (KANUPP)3 was supplied on a turnkey basis and became operational in 1972.

The KANUPP facility is natural uranium, heavy water reactor of the CANDU4 type, which according to some sources, can produce as much as 55 kg of plutonium per year.

In 1953, US President Dwight D Eisenhower envisioned the creation of this international body to control and develop the use of atomic energy, in his "*Atoms for Peace*" speech before the UN General Assembly. The IAEA (International Atomic Energy Agency) is the part of United Nations and it is world's centre of cooperation in the nuclear field. It was set up in July 29, 1957, its Secretariat headquartered at the Vienna International Centre in Vienna (Austria). The Agency works with its Member States (144 members) and multiple partners world-wide to promote safe, secure and peaceful nuclear technologies.

Pakistan's first nuclear energy plant (heavy-water, natural uranium, 137 MWe), Karachi Nuclear Power Plant (KANUPP) was realised with the help of Canada in 1972 under International Atomic Energy Agency (IAEA) safeguards.

The CANDU reactor is a Pressurised Heavy Water Reactor (PHWR) developed initially in the late 1950s and 1960s with partnership of Canada (Atomic Energy of Canada Limited-AECL), CANDU uses heavy water (deuterium oxide) for moderator and coolant, and natural uranium for fuel (4-6 bomb's worth) when operating at peak capacity. (Leventhal, *ORBIS*, spring 1992, p. 171).

However, the reactor has never operated at full capacity and since 1977 it was operating at a sharply reduced level due to a cut-off in Canadian fuel supplies. Pakistan then solicited bids for construction of a 900 MW light water, low enriched uranium fuelled power plant on the Indus River at Chashma5, where it could draw on hydroelectric power with the co-operation of China.

Zulfikar Ali Bhutto provided a new direction to Pakistan's nuclear policy in the 1960s, as Minister for Natural Resources and Atomic Energy and later as a Foreign Minister and demonstrated keen interest in nuclear weapons. Quite appropriately, an Indian scholar, Ashok Kapur, has stated that Bhutto "mobilised nuclear nationalism in Pakistan" (Kapur, 1987, p. 58). He declared in 1966 that if India built a nuclear bomb, Pakistan would follow suit, to retain a strategic balance with India, including the development of nuclear weapons, at any cost. In 1969, Bhutto wrote: "All wars of our age have become total wars...It would be dangerous to plan for less, and our plans should include the nuclear deterrent" (Brahma, 1993, p. 122). On January 1972 Bhutto held a secret meeting of the country's top scientists and engineers at Multan, where he committed his government to acquiring nuclear power and equipment (Spector, 1990, pp. 89-91). Bhutto attempted to purchase a reprocessing facility that would have enabled it to extract weapons-grade plutonium from spent nuclear fuel from France. Washington pressurised Paris and Islamabad into cancelling the deal, after which Pakistan clandestinely sought to acquire the technology to enrich uranium. In Pakistan, nuclear technology became linked to power, status and national security after an Indian nuclear test explosion in 1974. Bhutto, writing from his death cell in 1977, expressed this view: "We know that Israel and South Africa have full nuclear capability. The Christian, Jewish, and Hindu civilisations have this capability. The communist powers also possess it. Only the Islamic civilisation is without it, but that position is about to change".* (Bhutto, 1979, pp. 18 45).

After learning from intelligence reports that Pakistan is acquiring ability to make nuclear weapons, Carter Administration stopped all aid to Pakistan. This was done in accordance with an amendment of 'Nuclear Proliferation Act' which prohibited economic and military assistance to any country that obtained equipment for nuclear enrichment without placing it under internal safeguards (New York Times, April 7, 1979). Pakistan denied its plans to develop nuclear weapons and denounced the US decision to terminate American aid and suspicion that such nuclear programme was under way. It further attributed that the US policy was under the Zionist circles (New York Times, April 9, 1979).

It was held that Carter Administration's cut off economic aid to Pakistan for building their nuclear weapons plant, but no such action was taken against India by last three Adminis-

---

* Chashma Nuclear Power Plant is Pressurised Water Reactor (PWR) type. It is located near Chashma Barrage on the left bank of River Indus, 280 Kms from South West of Islamabad and 1160 Kms from North East of Karachi. It was designed and built by collaboration with China, and is being operated and maintained by Pakistan, this plant is delivering 300 Mew to the national grid since September 15, 2000.

trations for exploding the plutonium device; it was also known that 82-years old Indian Prime Minister Desai promised not to authorise second atomic test but his successors may not have felt that they were bound by any such promises (New York Times, April 16, 1979).

Carter Administration's plans to sell Pakistan up to 50 Northrop F-5E Tiger fighter planes - so as to give help on nuclear power to Pakistan; reach an agreement to restrict production of nuclear weapons; and offer diplomatic backing for controversial Pakistanis proposal and call for free nuclear zone in South Asia - reflected the Administration's growing concern over possibility of nuclear arms race between Pakistan and India. Some top officials' circles believed that Administration would have lost some leverage on Pakistan's nuclear plans by halting over $80 million in economic assistance (New York Times, April 17, 1979).

The US expressed concern that Pakistan quest for nuclear weapon capability could spark a nuclear arms race between India and Pakistan. But Pakistan continued to seek nuclear arms capacity despite US warnings (New York Times, February 28, 1980). President Zia-ul-Haq said Pakistan was determined to continue its nuclear programme for "peaceful purpose" because it was vital for country's economy (New York Times, March 11, 1980). The Reagan Administration did not believe that Pakistan had peaceful intention in continuing its nuclear programme. US Secretary of State, Alexander M Haig Junior favoured modification of legislation policy bars of aid to Pakistan because of its secret programme to develop nuclear devices, but the Reagan Administration sought to avoid isolating such countries as Pakistan so that they were not driven 'towards nuclear option' (New York Times, March 19, 1981). Representative Jonathan B Bingham opposed Haig's idea for change in Nuclear Non-Proliferation Act and contended that such action would send Pakistan a signal that it could develop nuclear weapons without risking its security relationship with the US (New York Times, March 19, 1981). Under Secretary James L Buckley defended Pakistan by saying that it had assured that it was neither developing nor planning to develop nuclear weapons (New York Times, June 25, 1981).

While the Reagan White House was considering billions of dollar of aid to Pakistan to buy its cooperation in fighting Soviet troops presence in Afghanistan. The US Senate voted to require annual report from President Reagan on policy on nuclear activity in Pakistan as a condition for renewal of military and economic aid (New York Times, October 21, 1981). US Senate, 51-46, votes required cut-off of the US foreign aid to Pakistan, if it detonated a nuclear device (New York Times, October 22, 1981). US Senate in course of debate on foreign aid bill also voted to allow resumption of economic and military aid to Pakistan, if the President report certified that Pakistan was not developing nuclear weapons (*ibid*).

In the mean time, US intelligence reported in January 1982 that Pakistan would be able to detonate nuclear device within next three years, but it was not likely to do so because of fear of jeopardising Reagan Administration's $3.2 billion military and economic aid programme (New York Times, January 26, 1982).

Then Pakistani Prime Minister Mohammad Khan Junejo, assured the Reagan Administration that Pakistan was not developing nuclear bomb (New York Times, July 17, 1986). State Depart-ment, concluded that Pakistan was probably involved in a plot to smuggle material for nuclear weapons out of United States, reportedly recommended that President Reagan waive law that would require cut off in aid to Pakistan (New York Times, January 14, 1988). Pakistani General Mirza Aslam Beg reported successful testing of two types of surface-to-surface missiles; also said Pakistan may produce its own tanks within two years (New York Times, February 6, 1988).

Bhutto's government was removed from power because the United States disapproved of his nuclear ambitions. He was a dynamic and outstanding politician and became a victim of opposition. He defied a superpower and, in the process, sacrificed his government and ultimately life itself and dedicated to national cause and survival. Thus, the Pakistani nuclear weapons programme took shape in 1976 when Dr Abdul Qadeer Khan, a German-trained metallurgist, returned to Pakistan from the Netherlands and ultimately, an enrichment facility at Kahuta, based on the stolen blueprints from Almelo gas centrifuge enrichment plant, was completed in 1985. Pakistan had also set up a small pilot plant at Sihala, the existence of which was acknowledged by Zia-ul-Haq. However, the Kahuta6 enrichment facility began to produce weapons-grade uranium in the Mid-1980s and this plant produced uranium enriched to more than the relatively innocuous five per cent level (*New York Times* (Magazine), March 6, 1988, p. 38). Thus, it was the uranium enrichment programme that provided the decisive breakthrough for Pakistan in the area of weapon-grade material production. The 1980s saw Pakistan's achievement of the target of designing a nuclear weapon and the acquisition of important hardware. Dr. Abdul Qadeer Khan, the mastermind behind the establishment of the Kahuta enriching plant, was able to announce his country's success in breaking the Western monopoly and Kahuta is Pakistan's main nuclear weapons laboratory as well as an emerging centre for long-range missile development. The primary Pakistani fissile-material production facility is located at Kahuta, employing gas centrifuge enrichment technology to produce Highly Enriched Uranium (HEU) exceeding the five per cent level in uranium enrichment (The New York Times, March 6, 1988).

Pakistan's crossing of the five per cent "red line" was not challenged by the United States because Pakistan was at that time a key ally, providing the crucial link in the CIA's effort to smuggle billions of dollars of weapons to Afghan guerrillas attempting to drive out the Soviet Union from Afghanistan (Smith, *New York Times* (Magazine). March 6, 1988). The Reagan administration was keen to supply Pakistan with sophisticated air-to-air missiles, and key congressional committees also approved US$ 3.2 billion five years (1981-1985) aid package to Pakistan (Omang, *Washington Post,* 21 March 1985). In March 1986, the Reagan administration announced that it would provide Pakistan a second six-year

(1985-1991) aid package worth of US$ 4.2 billion. From this point onward, the Reagan administration was aware that Pakistan had achieved capability to build nuclear arms or assemble the components (Boyd, *New York Times*, 17 July 1986). According to Milt Bearden (a senior CIA officer in Pakistan from 1986-1989), in the early 1986 the Soviets and Indians discussed Pakistan's nuclear issue with the US diplomats in an effort to isolate Pakistan from the Afghan issue but the US officials refused to discuss this matter and helped to create the conditions to produce weapons grade material (*New York Times*, 30 May 1998). According to the Tass report, the Reagan administration allowed Pakistan to increase their self-defence ability and Pakistan's nuclear capability was significantly improved during the years of 1985-86 in order to prevent the Soviets moving towards the Persian Gulf. During those years, Pakistan set up a worldwide smuggling ring to buy, copy or steal nuclear weapons technology. Some sources claimed that during this time, Pakistan conducted two nuclear tests and rapidly assembled at least one nuclear device in the event of a future war (Spector, 1990, p. 95). The Zia regime was completely successful in its clandestine efforts to secure classified designs of a centrifuge-based uranium enrichment plant and in obtaining a number of critical sub-systems, components and materials. Zia strongly supported Pakistan's nuclear programme and refused to accept full-scope safeguards. He said: "We shall eat crumbs but will not allow our national interest to be compromised in any manner what-so-ever". Zia admitted, "Pakistan can build a (nuclear) bomb whenever it wishes. Once you have acquired the technology, which Pakistan has, you can do whatever you like" (Doerner, *Time*, 30 March 1987, p. 42).

General Zia took risks, and skilfully exploited the international environment in the wake of the Afghan crisis. Although there was a lack of hard information concerning Pakistan's nuclear status, it was assumed that the country had the ability to manufacture atomic weapons and had become a de facto nuclear weapon state. An understanding of the historical and current sources of Pakistan's perception of the

US was critical to understanding as to why to Pakistan US nuclear policy was simply more evident of its duplicity and untrustworthiness. (Khan, *Strategic Insights*, Vol. 4, No., October 10, 2005, p. 2)

The US-Pak relationship had no strategic content during the 1970s, as new strains arose over Pakistan's efforts to respond to India's 1974 nuclear test by seeking its own nuclear capability. With the Soviet invasion of Afghanistan, however, US priorities shifted again, and Pakistan was again viewed as a frontline ally in the effort to block Soviet expansionism. In 1981, the Reagan Administration offered Islamabad a five-year, US$ 3.2 billion aid package, and turned a blind eye to Pakistan's nuclear programme and even waived specific sanctions mandated by law. (Alan Kronstadt, *CRS Issue Brief for Congress*, March 6, 2006, p. 3). The certification requirement was one in a series of linked non-proliferation sections of the Foreign Assistance Act (FAA)7 that attempted to use the threat of an aid cut off as an incentive to Pakistan to discontinue its efforts to acquire a nuclear weapons capability. The most pertinent provisions are noted below:

> The basic non-proliferation provision affecting Pakistan is Section 101 of the Arms Export Control Act (an expanded version of what was formerly Section 669 of the FAA). This provision forbids aid to countries that acquire nuclear enrichment facilities that are not under the inspection and safeguards system of the International Atomic Energy Agency (IAEA). The Carter Administration, in April 1979, invoked Section 669 and suspended aid to Pakistan after intelligence information confirmed that Pakistan was building a secret uranium enrichment facility.

Section 620E of the FAA, adopted by Congress in 1981 following the December 1979 Soviet invasion of Afghanistan, sought to reconcile US nuclear non-proliferation policy with urgent US regional security interests. Unlike Section 669, Section 620E8 is Pakistan-specific, having been adopted to reaffirm it.

The Foreign Assistance Act is a United States Act. FAA reorganised the US foreign assistance programmes and it separated military and non-military aid. It also mandated the creation of an agency to administer economic assistance programmes; on November 3, 1961, President John F. Kennedy established the U.S. Agency for International Development (USAID).

Section 620E of the FAA, adopted by the American Congress in 1981, Unlike Section 669, Section 620E is Pakistan-specific, having been adopted to reaffirm 1959 between the US-Pakistan bilateral security agreement and to permit the resumption of US military and economic assistance to Pakistan by granting authority to the President to waive Section 669 in Pakistan's case if the latter decides that to do so is in the national interest. The waiver authority was granted initially for a period of six years, facilitating the Reagan Administration's commitment of a six year, US$ 3.2 billion package of economic and military aid to Pakistan. The waiver authority was periodically extended by Congress after that date but subject to increasing conditions, especially the Section 620E (e) certification requirement. (http://www.ippnw-students.org/Chapters/Pakistan/Paknuke1.html).

References

Wolfers, Arnold (1962), National Security as an Ambiguous Symbol: Discord and Collaboration, Baltimore: John Hopkins University Press.

Buzan, Barry (1984), Peace, Power, and Security: Contending Concepts in the Study of International Relations, *Journal of Peace Research*, Vol. 21(2), pp.109-125 [online], http://jpr.sagepub.com/cgi/content/abstract/21/2/109.

Waltz, 1979, p. 168.

Handel, 1981, pp. 56-76.

Sorensen, *Security Dialogue*, p. 377.

Handel, 1981, p. 77.

Waltz, 1981, p. 30.

Thayer, *Security Studies,* 1995, pp. 150-155.

Morgenthau, *American Political Science Review*, 1964, p. 35 Kaiser, 1989, pp. 123-136.

Hoyt, 2005, pp. 113-115.

Pfaff, International Herald Tribune, 3 June 1998 Chellaney, *Survival*, Vol. 35, No. 3, autumn 1993, p. 122.

Leventhal, *ORBIS*, spring 1992, p. 171.

Kapur, 1987, p. 58.

Brahma, 1993, p. 122.

Spector, 1990, pp. 89-91.

Bhutto, 1979, pp. 18-45.

New York Times, April 9, 1979.

New York Times, April 16, 1979.

New York Times, April 17, 1979.

New York Times, February 28, 1980.

New York Times, March 11, 1980.

New York Times, March 19, 1981.

New York Times, March 19, 1981.

New York Times, June 25, 1981.

New York Times, October 21, 1981.

New York Times, October 22, 1981, *ibid.*

New York Times, January 26, 1982.

New York Times, July 17, 1986.

New York Times, January 14, 1988.

New York Times, February 6, 1988.

New York Times (Magazine), March 6, 1988, p. 38. The New York Times, March 6, 1988.

Smith, *New York Times* (Magazine) Omang, *Washington Post,* 21 March 1985 Boyd, *New York Times*, 17 July 1986, *New York Times*, 30 May 1998.

NotesNotes

Spector, 1990, p. 95.

Doerner, *Time*, 30 March 1987, p. 42.

Khan, *Strategic Insights*, Vol. 4, No., October 10, 2005, p. 2.

Alan, Kronstadt, *CRS Issue Brief for Congress*, March 6, 2006, p. 3.

Cronin, Richard P(1996), 90149: Pakistan Aid Cut off: U.S. Non proliferation and Foreign Policy Considerations, CRS, December 6, 1996[online], http://www.fas.org/spp/starwars/crs/90-149.htm

Afridi, Dr. Ali Raza Khan, IPPNW-Students Pakistan Pakistan Nuclear Weapons [online],http://www.ippnwstudents.org/Chapters/Pakistan/Paknuke1.ht ml

Chapter 5

Conclusion

US-Pak relations have had an extremely chequered history marked by ups and downs. Their bilateral relations constitute one of many contem-porary instances of an alliance serving complementary interests. For the United States it served primarily the purpose of expanding the scope of the policy of containment during the Cold War; for Pakistan it served the purpose of increasing political, military and economic potential vis-á-vis India.

In the immediate aftermath of the emergence of India and Pakistan as sovereign nations, American policy-makers approached South Asia primarily governed by British advice. American interest in sub-continental affairs was marginal. European economic recovery, the geopolitical requirements in the Middle East, and the containment of Soviet "expansionism" were accorded the greatest priority. Between India and Pakistan, however, Washington initially attached greater importance to the former apparently because it was larger in size and population, and had considerable economic and military potential. The relatively low level of American interest in Pakistan during 1947-49 was evident from tardiness in appointing an Ambassador to Pakistan.

As the Cold War unfolded, Pakistan leaned towards the West. Jinnah plainly spelled out that communism would not flourish in the soil of Islam. And that Pakistan's interests were more in common with the "two great democratic countries, namely, the UK and the USA, rather than with Russia". From the start, therefore, Pakistan's foreign policy orientation differed from that of India, which professed non-alignment. Practical considerations bolstered Pakistan's pro-western orientation. The financially strapped country badly needed help and was not bashful about seeking it from the United States.

When Eisenhower became President in 1953, US policy emphasised strengthening the collective security cordon around the communist bloc. In the case of South Asia, this meant enlisting Pakistan, which was only too willing, as a partner in bolstering the defence of the Middle East. Even though Washington realised that the move would strain relations with larger India, the step was deemed worthwhile. But the United States and Pakistan entered into the alliance for different and ultimately conflicting reasons. Despite its anti-communist rhetoric, Pakistan remained at heart concerned about the threat from India rather than any menace from the communists. In contrast, the United States saw the security accord with Pakistan as directed strictly against the communist threat and was wary of becoming entangled in Pakistan's dispute with India.

The announcement of military aid to Pakistan was made on 25 February 1954, i.e. soon after Pakistan demonstrated its "resolve to play an important part in the collective defence of the free world" by signing a friendship treaty with Turkey. The announcement of military aid was followed in quick succession by signing of the US-Pakistan Mutual Defence Agreement on 19 May 1954 and the formation of the South East Asia Treaty Organisation (SEATO) in September 1954 and the Baghdad Pact (CENTO) in 1955.

In 1959, Dwight Eisenhower became the first US President to visit Pakistan. Earlier, in the fall of 1959, Ayub Khan had announced measures designed to move his country slowly towards his version of democracy. He established a system of local councils, called "basic democracies", elected by universal suffrage. About eighty thousand "basic democrats" became a national electoral college that would select a national assembly in 1962 and elect a president in 1965. When Dwight Eisenhower left the White House in January 1961, he was happy that the US's South Asian ally, Pakistan, appeared to be getting on its feet under Ayub Khan and was beginning to make tangible economic progress. Many analysts saw that Pakistan was moving slowly from a military dictatorship towards the establishment of a relatively more open political system. Although the Pakistanis remained extremely unhappy about growing US support for India's economic development, the USPakistan bilateral relationship was growing too. The US continued to provide substantial economic and arms aid to Pakistan, including the promised supply of the controversial F-104 fighters. USPakistan ties were strained to some extent during the Kennedy Administration. President Kennedy wanted to improve ties with NAM countries, including India. Although Ayub did not oppose Kennedy's desire for better relations with non-aligned countries, such as India, he urged Washington to "maintain distinction between the non-aligned countries and Pakistan." He further stressed that the "focal point of Pakistan's policy was the continued friendship with the United States". He also indicated that he was trying to establish more normal relations with China and also with the Soviet Union. The Johnson years witnessed a fundamental shift in US-Pakistan relations. When Johnson became president after Kennedy's assassination, the bilateral relations were at a "standoff" over US military aid to India and Pakistan's flirtation with China. President Johnson sought to limit Pakistan's relationship with China at the price for continued large-scale US economic aid. When the pressure tactics failed and Pakistan and India went to war over Kashmir in 1965, Johnson largely gave up on Pakistan.

US-Pakistan relations had dramatically deteriorated during Kennedy and Johnson administrations. But when Richard Nixon moved into the White House, Islamabad had reason to hope for better days. An old friend of Pakistan, Nixon had visited the country five times, twice as Vice-President and three times after he left that office. Ayub had wisely given Nixon a red carpet during his travels as a private citizen. During 1971, the coincidence of the East Pakistan crisis and Nixon's China initiative placed South Asia at the centre of US foreign policy concerns. Tilting towards Pakistan, Nixon sought to protect the opening to China and to prevent what he feared would be a major Soviet gain in the balance of power in Asia. As a fundamental misreading of the India-Pakistan situation, Nixon's tilt towards Islamabad had little effect on the East Pakistan crisis but resulted in an embarrassing US diplomatic setback. President Nixon could do little to prevent the birth of a new nation, called Bangladesh.

The two and a half years of Gerald Ford's presidency saw a continuation of Nixon's policy of warm relations towards Pakistan. Even though Islamabad had left SEATO in 1972 and remained only a nominal member of CENTO, the Ford administration considered Pakistan a good friend and an ally.

The assumption of Presidency by Jimmy Carter in 1977 created apprehensions in Pakistan about the future of US-Pak relations because of his known unfavourable views on arms sales and nuclear proliferation. In fact, "tilt" towards Pakistan in the early 1970s gave way to the downward trend in the relations between the two countries which became even more evident during the Carter Administration and reached an all-time low in April 1979.

Following the Soviet invasion of Afghanistan in December 1979, however, Pakistan came to be viewed as a frontline state against Soviet expansionism. Earlier, Pakistan had little involvement in Afghanistan, accepting, as did the US, that it was on the margins of the Soviet sphere of influence. However, following the Soviet invasion of Afghanistan, Pakistan's then military regime eagerly accepted Washington's demand that Pakistan serve as the frontline state in what eventually proved to be the last great Cold War confrontation.

When the Soviets invaded Afghanistan in 1979, for the first time in its history, Pakistan faced an extra regional threat at its doorstep. The US alliance, designed for such a contingency, finally came through, and massive amounts of US aid and equipment were moved into Pakistan as has been discussed earlier, to face off the Soviet threat. Pakistan could not defend itself from the Soviet forces conventionally, let alone defeat them. It decided, however, to work with the United States to support guerrillas (Mujahidin) in Afghanistan who could take the fight to the Soviets asymmetrically.

The United States and Saudi Arabia poured money into Afghan Islamic groups through Pakistan, to fight the anti-Soviet jihad. While Pakistan and the United States were locked in proxy conflict with the Soviets over Afghanistan, Pakistan turned out to be an invaluable ally. Despite Islamabad's progress in pursuing a secret nuclear weapon programme, US economic and military aid continued to flow to support the anti-Soviet campaign. US dissuasive policy against nuclear development was designed around the belief that a conventionally well-armed Pakistan would not pursue the nuclear track aggressively (*ibid*). But unlike in the past, this time around Pakistan benefited a great deal from massive US military and economic assistance in the wake of the Afghanistan crisis.

It is clear that both the United States and Pakistan mutually benefited from a new strategic alliance aimed at making the Soviet military presence politically costly, economically expensive and militarily untenable. Had there been no Soviet invasion of Afghanistan, Pakistan would have been rotting under a military regime and international sanctions due to its secret nuclear weapon programme.

The Afghanistan crisis of the 1980s brought, according to Chintamani Mahapatra, unprecedented economic benefits, political capital, and militarily benefits to Pakistan (for details see *Strategic Analysis,* Vol. XIX-No.7).

Though Pakistan was able to build up with US assistance its conventional military capabilities aimed at matching Indian conventional superiority, its cooperation with the Reagan Administration would not have enabled the US to win the Cold War by forcing the Soviet Union to withdraw its force from Afghanistan.

The CIA and the ISI, the Pentagon and the Pakistani militarily establishment, and the Reagan White House and the Zia regime were able to forge a kind of strategic cooperation in strengthening the anti-Soviet attacks and operations by the Afghan Mujahidin that finally forced Soviet leader Mikhail Gorbachev to conclude a deal with the President Reagan in 1987.

This deal was about the complete withdrawal of the Soviet military force from the Afghan territory. It is not an exaggeration to say that the Soviet debacle in Afghanistan was instrumental in ending the Cold War. It can also be said that the Soviet intervention in Afghanistan was responsible to a great extent for the eventual collapse of the Soviet Union.

The role of the United States, particularly the eight years of the Reagan Administration, was significant in the victory of West in the Cold War. In this, the role of Pakistan, especially the military regime led by General Zia-ul-Haq, cannot be under-estimated. However, it would not be appropriate to give too much credit to the Zia regime, because unlike the goal of the Reagan Administration, Pakistan never aimed at winning the Cold War. Islamabad considered India as the main enemy. It could not forget India's role in the creation of Bangladesh by dividing Pakistan; and sought to build up its military strength by cooperating with the US.

Pakistanis understood that the Soviet Union stood behind India during the 1971 Indo-Pakistani war. When the Soviet Union sent its troops to Afghanistan and established a puppet regime, Pakistan knew that the US would seek its help in containing Soviet expansionism. Gen. Zia aimed at taking advantage of this situation to improve Pakistan's militarily capabilities vis-á-vis India. Thus, Washington's goal and Pakistan's objective were different. But both the parties got considerable benefit out of a decade of alliance relationship, a sort of temporary marriage of convenience.

The most important strategic game of Pakistan was the upgradation of its conventional arsenal and acquisition of nuclear weapon capability. The nuclear gain of Pakistan, however, was at the cost of Washington's non-proliferation policy and objectives. Ever since India conducted its peaceful nuclear explosion, successive US Administrations adopted strong non-proliferation policy, took the lead in establishing international regimes and set up export control mechanisms.

The Reagan Administrations did not implement the non-proliferations goal and policy during the Afghan crisis. Had it done so, Pakistan could never have acquired the nuclear weapon capability. During both his terms, President Reagan and his foreign policy advisors gave top priority to fight against the Soviet military presence in Afghanistan. Since, Pakistan was a very important link in American strategy against the Soviet military intervention in Afghanistan, the Reagan Administration did not put any pressure on Pakistan to stop its secret activities for acquiring nuclear weapon capability.

As we have discussed in Chapter IV, Pakistani leaders were prepared to feed their people with grass, it was that necessary to get a nuclear bomb. Pakistan was lucky that it could successfully achieve a nuclear weapon capability, while receiving huge amount of American economic assistance. The Reagan Administration was aware that the US Congress strongly supported the nuclear non-proliferation measures, and in 1985 enacted the Pressler Amendment. This measure was taken in the wake of US intelligence's finding that Pakistan was deeply involved in secret activities to buy nuclear weapon related equipment from the international market.

The Reagan White House did not impose any sanction on Pakistan under the Pressler Amendment. On the other hand, it requested the Congress to approve military assistance of sophisticated weapons on the ground that it would discourage Pakistan from seeking nuclear weapon capability. The regional implication of the Reagan Administration's policy, however, was negative in many ways. First, the acquisi-tion of nuclear weapon capability by Pakistan through illegal means, which was known to the Reagan Administration, led to the erosion of credibility of the US non-proliferation policy.

Secondly, massive amount of American assistance to Pakistan encouraged corruption in many ways. In fact, many American weapons sent for Afghan Mujahidin never reached them. A huge number of unaccounted American weapons were spread across the Pakistani society and let to the militarisation of social life.

Thirdly, the CIA-ISI collaboration was responsible to a considerable extent for drugs production, marketing and abuse. At first, narcotics addiction was confined to the locality, but eventually it spread across the region and then became an international security threat. But for the CIA help, the

ISI would not have become powerful enough to behave like a state within a state. The root cause of rise of the Taliban and deadly terrorist activities witnessed today goes back to the ISI activism during the Afghan crisis.

Bibliography

A. Primary Sources

Government Documents/Publications:

Amnesty International Report (1986), London: Amnesty International Publications, pp. 246-249.

Brzezinski, Zbigniew (1983), Power and Principle: Memoirs of the National Security Adviser, 1977-1981, New York: Farrar, Straus, Giroux, pp. 429, 432, 444, 448-449.

Congressional Hearings (1980), 86th Congress, 1st Session, House Committee on Foreign Affairs, Subcommittee on Asian and Pacific Affairs, Hearings, *Crisis in the Sub-continent, Afghanistan and Pakistan,* (U.S. Government Printing Office: Washington D.C.).

........,,(1982), 88th Congress, 2nd Session, House Committee on Foreign Affairs, Subcommittee on Inter-national Economic Policy and Trade, Hearings, *Scourity and Economic Assistance to Pakistan*, (U.S. Government Printing Office: Washington D.C.).

........,,(1992), 98th Congress, 1st Session, Senate, Committee on Foreign Relations, Hearings, *The Pressler Amendment and Pakistan's Nuclear Weapons Programme*, July 30, 1992 (U.S. Government Printing Office: Washington D.C.).

Cronin, Richard P. and Barbara Leitch LePoer. (1993), "*South Asia: US Interests and Policy Issues*" *CRS Issue Brief for Congress No. 93-243F*, Congressional Research Service (CRS), February 12, 1993, Library of Congress: Washington D.C.

Doan, Michael (August 25, 1986), "Daughter on a Pakistan Power Trip," *US News and World Report*.

"FY 1987, Assistance Requests for South Asia," Department of State Bulletin, July 1986, "Visit of Pakistan's Prime Minister," Department of State Bulletin (October 1986).

Grimmett, Richard F. (1999), "Foreign Policy Roles of the President and Congress", Congressional Research Service (CRS), June 1, 1999 Library of Congress: Washington, D.C.

LePoer, Barbara Leitch (June 16, 1994) *"Pakistan-U.S. Relations", CRS Issue Brief for Congress No. IB9404*, Congressional Research Service (CRS), Library of Congress: Washington D.C.

Taylor, Walter A. and Peter Ross Range (September 1, 1986), "Pakistan's Violent Turn," *U.S. News and World Report*.

US Congress. *Congressional Record*. 1947-1965.

US Department of State *Bulletin*. 1947-1965.

US Department of State. *Foreign Relations of the United States*, 1947-1961.

US House of Representatives, Committee on Foreign Affairs (February , 1951), *India Emergency Assistance Act of 1951: Hearings*.

US House of Representatives, Committee on Foreign Affairs. *Selected Executive Session Hearings* (Historical Series).

US Senate, Committee on Foreign Relations. *Executive Sessions of the Senate Foreign Relations Committee* (Historical Series).

United States Department of Commerce (1992), International Trade Administration. *Foreign Economic Trends and Their Implications for the United States: Pakistan*. (FET92-09.) (U.S. Government Printing Office: Washington D.C.).

United States International Security and Science (1989), House Committee on Foreign Affairs, Subcommittee on Arms Control, *The Proposed Sale of F-16's to Pakistan*, (US Government Printing Office: Washington D.C.).

United States. Department of Commerce. International Trade Administration (April, 1992), *Foreign Economic Trends and Their Implications for the United States: Pakistan*, (FET92-09.) Washington.

United States. Department of State (1992), *International Narcotics Control Strategy Report*. Washington: GPO.

United States. Department of State (1993), *Country Reports on Human Rights Practices for 1992*, Report submitted to United States Congress, 103d, 1st Session, Senate, Committee on Foreign Relations, and House of Representatives, Committee on Foreign Affairs, Washington: GPO.

United States. Department of State (1994), *Country Reports on Human Rights Practices for 1993*, Report submitted to United States Congress, 103d, 2d Session, House, Committee on Foreign Affairs, and Senate, Committee on Foreign Relations, Washington: GPO.

Weisman (1977), "Struggle in Pakistan," Amnesty International, An Amnesty International Report Including the Findings of a Mission to Pakistan, p. 43, 23 April - 12 May.

Memoirs

Benson, Michael (2003), *Ronald Reagan (Presidential Letters)*, Lerner Publishing Group: Minneapolis, MN.

Eisenhower, Dwight D. (1965), *The White House Years: Waging Peace*, 1952-1961 Doubleday: Garden City, New York.

Gates, Robert (The former director of the CIA),"From the Shadows."

House Shultz, George P. (1993), Turmoil and Triumph: My Years as Secretary of State, New York, NY: Scribner.

Khan, Mohammed Ayub (1967), *Friends Not Maters: A Political Autobiography,* New York, Oxford University Press.

Kissinger Henry A (1979), *The White House Years*, New Delhi: Vikas.

Morris, Edmund (1999), *Dutch: A Memoir of Ronald Reagan*, New York: Random.

Nixon, Richard (1978), *RN: The Memories of Richard Nixon,* New York: Grosset and Dunlop.

Reagan, Nancy (1989), My Turn: The Memoirs of Nancy Reagan, New York: Harper Collins.

.... Ronald (1990), An American Life, New York: Simon and Schuster

Taseer, Salmaan (1979), *Bhutto: A Political Biography*. London: Ithac.

Truman, Harry S. (1956), *Memories: Years of Trial and Hope*, (Three Volumes), (Garden City, N.Y.: Doubleday).

B. Secondary Sources

Books

Abbott, Freeland (eds) (1966), "Pakistan and the Secular *State."* in Donald E. Smith. *South Asian Politics and Religion.* Princeton: Princeton University Press.

.......(1968), *Islam and Pakistan.* Ithaca: Cornell University Press, United States.

Adams, Charles J. (eds) (1966), "The Ideology of Mawlana Maududi." in Donald E. Smith, *South Asian Politics and Religion.* Princeton: Princeton University Press.

Afzal, M. Rafique (1976), *"Political Parties in Pakistan, 1947-1958",* Islamabad: National Commission on Historical and Cultural Research.

Ali, Chaudhri Mohammed (1967), *The Emergence of Pakistan.* New York: Columbia University Press.

Azfar, Kamal (1991), "Constitutional Dilemmas in Pakistan." Pages 49-85 in Shahid Javed Burki and Craig Baxter, *Pakistan under the Military: Eleven Years of Zia-ul-Haq.* Boulder, Colorado: Westview Press.

Azmi, M. Raziullah, (ed.) (1994), *Pakistan American Relations: The Recent Past*, Karachi: Royal Book Company.

Barnds, William J (1972), *India, Pakistan, and the Great Powers*. New York: Praeger.

Baxter, Craig (1985), *Zia's Pakistan: Politics and Stability in a Frontline State*. Boulder, Colorado: Westview Press, in Baxter, Craig, and Syed Razi Wasti, *Pakistan Authoritarianism in the 1980s,* Lahore: Vanguard.

.... (1991), "The United States and Pakistan: The Zia Era and the Afghan Connection" in Daniel Pipes and Adam Garfinkle, eds., *Friendly Tyrants: An American Dilemma*. New York: St. Martin's Press.

.... (1991) "Pakistan Becomes Prominent in the International Arena." in Shahid Javed Burki and Craig Baxter, *Pakistan under the Military: Eleven Years of Zia-ul- Haq*. Westview Press: Boulder, Colorado.

........and Syed Razi Wasti, eds. (1991), *Pakistan Authoritarianism in the 1980s*. Lahore: Vanguard.

Betts, Richard K., (ed.) (2002), Conflict After the Cold War: Arguments on Causes of War and Peace, New York: Orient Longman.

Brand William J. (1972), *India, Pakistan and the Great Powers*, New York: Praeger.

Brown, W. Norman (1967), *The United States and India and Pakistan* (New York: Oxford University Press.

Burk, S. M. (1974), *Mainspring of Indian and Pakistani Foreign Policies*, Minneapolis University of Minnesota Press.

.... and Lawrence Ziring (1998), *Pakistan's Foreign Policy: An Historical Analysis.* Hill and Wang: New York.

.... (1991), *Pakistan: The Continuing Search for Nationhood*, Westview Press: Boulder Colorado.

.... and Craig Baxter (eds) (1991), *Pakistan under the Military: Eleven Years of Zia-ul-Haq B.*, Westview Press: Boulder, Colorado.

Busch, Andrew E. (2005), Reagan's Victory: The Presidential Election of 1980 and the Rise of the Right, Lawrence,

Birdwood, Lord (1954), *India and Pakistan: A Continent Decides*. New York: Praeger.

Blinkenberg (1972), *India-Pakistan: The History of Unsolved Conflicts.* Copenhagen: Munksgaard.

Bose, Suyata (1990), *South Asia and World Capitalism*. New Delhi: Oxford University Press.

Brands, H. W. (1989), *The Specter of Neutralism: The United States and the Emergence of the Third World,* (1947-1960). New York: Columbia University Press.

.........., (1990), *India and the United States: The Cold Peace.* Boston: Twayne.

Brines, Russell (1968), *The Indo-Pakistan Conflict*. London: Paul Mall Press.

Burke, S. M. (1974), *Mainsprings of Indian and Pakistani Foreign Policies*. Minneapolis: University of Minnesota Press.

.... (1979), *Pakistan's Foreign Policy: An Historical Analysis.* London: Oxford University Press.

Burki, Shahid Javed and Craig Baxter (eds)(1991), *Pakistan under the Military: Eleven Years of Zia-ul-Haq*, Boulder, Colorado, Westview Press.

Buzan, Barry and Gowher Rizvi, (eds) (1986), *South Asian Insecurity and the Great Powers.* New York: St. Martin's.

Campagna, Anthony S. (1994), The Economy in the Reagan Years: The Economic Consequences of the Reagan Administrations, Westport, CT: Greenwood Press.

Cannon, Lou (1991), President Reagan: The Role of a Lifetime, New York: Simon and Schuster.

.... (2000), President Reagan: The Role of a Lifetime, New York: Public Affairs.

..........Michael Beschloss (2001), Ronald Reagan: The Presidential Portfolio: A History Illustrated from the Collection of the Ronald Reagan Library and Museum, Texas: Public Affairs.

Callard, Keith (1957), *Pakistan: A Political Study*. London: Allen and Unwind.

Chari, P.R. (1995), *Indo-nuclear Standoff: The Role of the United States*, New Delhi: Manohar publications.

Cheema, Pervaiz Iqbal (1990), *Pakistan's Defence Policy, 1947-58*, Basingstoke, United Kingdom, Macmillan.

Chopra, Surendra, (1983), *Perspectives on Pakistan's Foreign Policy*. Amritsar: Guru Nanak Dev University Press.

Choudhury, G. W. (1975), *India, Pakistan, Bangladesh, and the Major Powers: Politics of a Divided Subcontinent*. New York: Free Press.

.........., (1975), *The Last Days of United Pakistan*, Bloomington: Indiana University Press.

Clawson, Robert W. (1986), *East-West Rivalry in the Third World: Security Issues and Regional Perspectives*. Wilmington: Scholarly Resources.

Cohen, Stephen P. (1984), *The Pakistan Army*. Berkeley: University of California Press.

........(1987), *The Security of South Asia: Asian and American Perspectives,* Chicago: University of Illinois Press.

........(1987), *The Security of South Asia*, Urbana: University of Illinois Press.

Coll, Steve, (2004), Ghost Wars: The Secret History of the CIA, Afghanistan, and Bin Laden, from the Soviet Invasion to September 10, 2001, Penguin Books: New York.

Dallek, Matthew (2004), The Right Moment: Ronald Reagan's First Victory and the Decisive Turning Point in American Politics, New York: Oxford University Press

Diego Cordovez and Selig Harrison (eds) (1995), *Out of Afghanistan*, New York University Press: New York.

Diggins, John Patrick (2007), Ronald Reagan: Fate, Freedom, and the Making of History, New York: W. W. Norton.

D'Souza, Dinesh (1997), Ronald Reagan: How an Ordinary Man Became an Extraordinary Leader, New York: Free Press.

Ehrman, John (2005), The Eighties: America in the Age of Reagan, New Haven, CT: Yale University Press.

Eliot, Theodore, and Robert Pfaltzgraff (eds) (1986), *The Red Army on Pakistan's Borders: Implications for the United States*, Washington: Pergamon-Brassey's.

Frankel, Francine R. (1986), "Play the India Card," *Foreign Policy* (Spring).

Freidel, Frank; Hugh Sidey (eds) (1995), The Presidents of the United States of America, Washington D.C.: White House Historical Association.

Galambos, Louis (ed) (1989), *The Papers of Dwight Eisenhower*, Vol. (12). Baltimore: Johns Hopkins University Press.

Ganguly, Sumit (1986), *The Origins of the War in South Asia*, Boulder: Westview Press.

Ganguly, Shivaji (1990), *US Policy towards South Asia* (Boulder, Colorado: Westview Press.

Garthoff, Raymond L. (ed.) (1994), *Detente and Confrontation: American-Soviet Relations from Nixon to Reagan*, Brookings Institution Press: Washington D.C.

Gerald, Frances Fitz (2000), Way Out There in the Blue: Reagan, Star Wars, and the End of the Cold War, New York: Simon and Schuster.

Gupta, R. C. (1977), *US Policy towards India and Pakistan*, New Delhi: R. publication.

Harrison, Selig S (1981), *In Afghanistan's Shadow: Baluch Nationalism and Soviet Temptations.* New York: Carnegie Endowment for International Peace.

Heandel, Dan (1977), The Process of Priority Formulation: US Foreign Policy in Indo- Pakistan War of 1971, Boulder: Westview Press.

Heeger, Gerald (1980), "After the Tilt: The Making of US Foreign Policy towards Pakistan, 1972-1974." in Lloyd I. Rudolph and Susanne Hoeber Rudolph, *The Regional*

Imperative: US Foreign Policy Towards South Asian States. New Delhi, Concept.

Hersh, Seymour (1983), The Price of Power: Kissinger to Nixon in the White House, New York: Summit Books.

Hertsgaard, Mark. (1988), On Bended Knee: The Press and the Reagan Presidency, New York: Farrar Straus and Giroux.

Husain, Noor A., and Leo Rose (eds) (1988), *Pakistan-US Relations: Social, Political and Economic Factors*, Berkeley: Institute of East Asian Studies.

Ispahani, Mahnaz (1990), *Pakistan: The Dimensions Insecurity*, London; Brassey's for international Institute of Strategic Digest.

Jain, Rashmi (1983), *US-Pak Relations: 1947-1983*, New Delhi: Radiant.

James, William, and Subroto Roy, eds.(1992), *Foundations of Pakistan's Political Economy: Towards an Agenda for the 1990s*, Newbury Park, California: Sage.

Jillani, Anees (ed) (1993), Judicial Activism and Islamisation after Zia: Toward the Prohibition of Riba, in Charles H. Kennedy, Pakistan: 1992. Boulder, Colorado: Westview Press.

Johnson, Rob (2005), *A Region in Turmoil: South Asian Conflicts Since 1947*, London: Reaktion Books.

Jones, Rodney W. (1981), *Nuclear proliferation: Islam, the bomb and the South Asia*, Beverly Hills: Centre for Strategic and International Studies, Georgetown University.

Joshi, Manoj (1999), *The lost of Rebellion: Kashmir in the Nineties,* New Delhi: Penguine.

Kengor, Paul and Peter Schweizer (eds) (2005), The Reagan Presidency: Assessing the Man and His Legacy, Lanham, MD: Rowman and Littlefield.

Khalid Mahmud Arif (1995), *Working with Zia,* Karachi, Oxford University Press.

Khan, Tufail Ahmad (1989), "*Glimpses of Pakistan Econom 1980-88*", Karachi, Business Research and Service Institute.

Kissinger, Henry (1979), *White House Years,* Boston: Little, Brown and Company.

Kolko, Gabriel. (1988), "Confronting the Third World: United States Foreign Policy", 1945-1980, New York: Pantheon.

Korbal, Josef (1954), *Danger in Kashmir*, Princeton, Princeton University Press.

Kux, Dennis (1993), *Estranged Democracies: India and The United States, 1941-1991,* New Delhi: Sage Publication.

.... (2001), *The United States and Pakistan 1947-2000: Disenchanted Allies,* New York: Oxford University Press.

Kwitny, Jonathan (1984), Endless Enemies: The Making of an Unfriendly World, New York: Congdon and Weed.

LaFeber, Walter (2002), America, Russia, and the Cold War, 1945-1971, New York: Wiley.

Lamb, Alister, (1966), *The Kashmir Problem*, New York: Praeger

Leffler, Melvyn P. (1992), A Preponderance of Power; National Security, The Truman Administration, and the Cold War, Sandford: Sandford University Press.

Leo, E.Rose and Noor A. Hussain (1987), *United State and Pakistan forum: Relations with the major powers*, Lahaur.

Macdonald, Douglas J. (1992), *Adventures in Chaos: American Inter-vention for Reform in the Third World.* Cambridge, Mass.: Harvard University Press.

Malik, Iftikhar M (1992), US-South Asian Relations, 1940-47: American Attitudes towards the Pakistan Movement, New York: St. Martin's Press.

Martin, Anderson (1990), Revolution: The Reagan Legacy, Stanford, CA: Hoover Institution Press, Stanford University.

Matlock, Jack (2004), Reagan and Gorbachev: How the Cold War Ended, New York: Random House.

McMahon, Robert J. (1994), The Cold War on the Periphery: The United States: India and Pakistan, New York: Columbia University Press.

Melanson, Richard A (2001), American Foreign Policy since the Vietnam War: The Search for Consensus from Nixon to Clinton, M.E. Sharpe: New York.

Mosshaver, Z (1991), Nuclear weapons Proliferation in the Indian Subcontinent, London; Macmillan.

Muttam, John (1974), US, Pakistan and India: A Study of US Role of India-Pakistan arms race, New Delhi: Sindhu publications.

Norman, Omar (1988), *The Political Economy of Pakistan, 1947-85.* London: KPI.

Oldenburg, Philip (eds) (1980), *The Breakup of Pakistan*, in Lloyd I. Rudolph and Susanne Hoeber Rudolph, *The Regional Imperative: US Foreign Policy Towards South Asian States.* New Delhi: Concept.

Pakistan Bar Council (1982), Report on the Proposed Establishment of Courts of Qazis Ordinance, Lahore.

Palmer, Norman D. (1966), *South Asia and United States Policy.* Boston: Houghton Mifflin.

Palmer, Norman D. (1977), "*Pakistan: The Long Search for Foreign Policy*" in Lawrence Ziring, Ralph Braibanti, and W. Howard Wriggins, eds., *Pakistan: The Long View*, North Carolina: Durham, Duke University Press.

Paterson, Thomas G. (1988), *Meeting the Communist Threat: Truman to Reagan*, New York: Oxford University Press.

.........., (1977), *Pakistan: The Long Search for Foreign Policy*, in Lawrence Ziring, Ralph Braibanti, and W. Howard Wriggins, *Pakistan: The Long View.* Durham, North Carolina: Duke University Press.

Qasir, Nadeem (1991), *Pakistan Studies: An Investigation into the Political Economy, 1948-1988,* Karachi, Oxford University Press.

Rajan, M. S., and Shivaji Ganguly, (eds) (1981), *Great Power Relations, World Order, and the Third World.* New Delhi: Vikas.

Rahman, Ataur (1982), *Pakistan and America: dependency Relations*, New Delhi: Young Asia Publications.

Ray, Aswini K. (1975), Domestic Compulsions and Foreign Policy: Pakistan in Indo-Soviet Relations. Delhi: Manas.

Reeves, Richard (2005), President Reagan: The Triumph of Imagination, New York: Simon and Schuster.

Riaz Mohammed Khan (1991), *Untying the Afghan Knot: Negotiating the Soviet Withdrawal*, Durham: Duke University Press.

Riza, Shaukat (1984), *The Pakistan Army, 1: War 1965.* Lahore: Army Education Press.

.........,(1990), *The Pakistan Army, 2: 1966-71.* Lahore: Services Book Club.

Rizvi, Hasan-Askari (1988), *The Military and Politics in Pakistan,* Konark: New Delhi.

........., (1993), *Pakistan and Geostrategic Environment*, New York: St. Martin's Press.

Rose, Leo and Noor Huisain, (eds) (1985), *United States-Pakistan Relations,* Berkeley: Vanguard Institute of East Asian Studies.

Rose, Leo, and Kamal Matinuddin (eds) (1989), *Beyond Afghanistan: The Emerging US-Pakistan Relations.* Berkeley: Institute of East Asian Studies.

........., and Kamal Matinuddin (1989), *Beyond Afghanistan: The Emerging US- Pakistan Relations,* Berkeley: Institute of East Asian Studies.

Rudolph, Lloyd I., and Susanne Hoeber Rudolph (eds) (1980), The Regional Imperative: The Administration of US Foreign Policy Towards South Asian States under Presidents Johnson and Nixon, N.J: Atlantic Highlands, Humanities Press.

Sayeed, Khalid B (1967), *The Political System of Pakistan.* Boston: Houghton Mifflin.

.........., (1980), *Politics in Pakistan: The Nature and Direction of Change.* New York: Praeger.

.........., (1982), "The Historical Origins of Some of Pakistan's Persistent Political Problems", in A. Jayarat-nam Wilson and Dennis Dalton, *The States of South Asia: Problems of National Integration.* New Delhi: Vikas.

Schell, Jonathan (1994), Victory: The Reagan Administration's Secret Strategy That Hastened the Collapse of the Soviet Union, New York: Atlantic Monthly Press.

Schweizer, Peter (2002), Reagan's War: The Epic Story of His Forty Year Struggle and Final Triumph over Communism, New York: Doubleday.

.........., (1982), The United States and Pakistan; The Evolution of an Influence relationship, New York: Praeger.

Singh, Jasjit (1999), *Kargil: Pakistan's Fourth War for Kashmir*, New Delhi: Knowledge World.

Sisson, Richard, and Leo E. Rose, (eds) (1990), *War and Secession: Pakistan, India, and the Creation of Bangladesh.* Berkeley: University of California Press.

Sherwani, Latif Ahmed (1980), *Pakistan, China, and America,* Karachi: Council for Pakistan Studies.

Spector, Leonard S (1985), *The New Nuclear Nations*, New York: Vintage Books.

.........., (1988), *Nuclear Weapons and South Asian Security,* Washington D.C.: Carnegie Endowment for International Peace.

Steve, Coll, (2004), Ghost Wars: The Secret History of the CIA, Afghanistan, and Bin Laden, from the Soviet Invasion to September 10, 2001, New York: Penguin Books.

Tahir-Kheli, Shirin (1982), *The United States and Pakistan: The Evolution of an Influence Relationship,* New York: Praeger.

.........., (1997), *India, Pakistan and the United States: Breaking with the Pas,* New York: Council of Foreign Relations.

Taseer, Salmaan (1979), *Bhutto: A Political Biography.* London: Ithaca.

Thornton, Thomas P. (1987), *Pakistan: Internal Developments and the US Interest,* Washington D.C.: Foreign Policy Institute.

United States (1991), Department of State, Bureau of International Narcotics Matters.

.... (1992), Embassy in Islamabad. *Health and Medical Information.* January.

Venkataramani, M. S. (1982), *The American Role in Pakistan, 1947-1958.* New Delhi: Radiant.

Walsh, Kenneth (1997), *Ronald Reagan,* New York: Random House Value Publishing, Inc.

Waseem, Mohammad (1987), *"Pakistan under Martial Law, 1977-1985"* Lahore, Vanguard.

Wilcox, Wayne A. (1963), *Pakistan: The Consolidation of a Nation.* New York: Columbia University Press.

Wills, Garry (2000), *Reagan's America,* New York: Penguin Books.

Winik, Jay (1996), *On the Brink: The Dramatic, Behind-the-Scenes Saga of the Reagan Era and the Men and Women Who Won the Cold War,* New York: Simon and Schuster.

Wriggins, W. Howard (1977), *The Balancing Process in Pakistan's Foreign Policy,* in Lawrence Ziring, Ralph Braibanti, and W. Howard Wriggins, *Pakistan: The Long View.* Durham, North Carolina: Duke University Press.

Wirsing, Robert G (1989), Pakistan's Security under Zia, 1977-1988: The Policy Imperatives of a Peripheral Asian State. New York: St. Martin's Press.

Wirsing, Robert G (1991), *Pakistan's Security under Zia, 1977-1988: The Policy Imperatives of a Peripheral Asian State.* New York: St. Martin's Press.

Wolpert, Stanley. *Jinnah of Pakistan.* New York: Oxford University Press, 1984.

.... (1982), *Roots of Confrontation in South Asia: Afghanistan, Pakistan, India and the Superpowers.* New York: Oxford University Press.

Yusuf, Hamid (1980), *Pakistan in Search of Democracy, 1947-77,* Lahore: Afrasia.

Ziring, Lawrence S. (1971), *The Ayub Khan Era: Politics in Pakistan, 1958-69.* Syracuse, N.Y.: Syracuse University Press.

Ziring, Lawrence (1977), *Pakistan: The Long View.* Durham: Duke University Press.

.... (1980), *Pakistan: The Enigma of Political Development.* Boulder, Colorado: Westview.

.... (1982) *The Subcontinent in the World Politics: India, its Neighbors and the Great Powers,* New York: Praeger.

Articles

Afroz, Sultana (1994), "Cold War and United States Military Aid to Pakistan, 1947-1960: A Reassessment", *South Asia* (New South Wales), 17(1).

Ahmad, Samina, (1999), "Nuclearisation of South Asia and Kashmir Dispute", *Regional Studies*, Islamabad (summer).

Ali, Mehrunnisa, (1979), "Pakistan-United States Relations: The Recent Phase", *Pakistan Horizon* (Karachi), Vol. 2 (3).

Ayoob, Mohammed (1985), "Dateline Pakistan: A Passage to Anarchy?" *Foreign Policy* (Summer 1985).

Ayub Khan, Mohammed (1964), "The Pakistan-American Alliance: Stresses and Strains." *Foreign Affairs*, Vol. 42.

Bose, T. C. (March, 1994), "The United States and South Asia: The Nuclear Proliferation Dimension", *Strategic Analysis*, Vol.16, no.12.

Brands, H. W. Jr. (1986), "India and Pakistan in American Strategic Planning, 1947-1957: Commonwealth as

Collaborator", *Journal of Imperial and Commonwealth History*, Vol. 15.

Broad, William J., David E. Sanger, and Raymond Bonner (12 February, 2004), "A Tale of Nuclear Proliferation: How a Pakistani Built His Network". *New York Times.*

Burki, Shahid Javed (October, 1988), "Pakistan under Zia, 1977-1988," *Asian Survey*, Vol. 28, No.10.

Carpenter, Ted Galen (5 January, 1987), "A Fortress Built on Quicksand: US Policy toward Pakistan", Policy Analysis, Vol. 80.

Carrington, Tim (16 October, 1986), "Zia Seeks US Radar, Anti-aircraft Guns to Blunt Afghan Forays into Pakistan," *Wall Street Journal.*

Chadda, Maya, (October-December, 1981), "Super Power Rivalry in South West Asia: The Afghan Crisis 1979", *India Quarterly*, New Delhi, Vol. 37(4).

.........,(1976), " US Weapons and South Asia: A Policy Analysis", *Pacific Affairs*, Vancouver, 49 (1).

Cheema, Pervaiz Iqbal (March, 1983), "The Afghanistan Crisis and Pakistan Dilemma", *Asian Survey*, 23 (3), March.

Christopher, Layne (1985-1986), "The Real Conservative Agenda," *Foreign Policy* (Winter).

Clifton, Tony (21 April, 1986), "Challenging General Zia," *Newsweek.*

Gaan, Narottam, (October-November, 1990), "Superpower Involvement in India-Pakistan Relations", *India Quarterly,* Vol. 46(4).

Ganguly, Sumit, (December, 1990), "Deterrence Failure Revisited; The Indo-Pakistan War of 1965," *Journal of Strategic Studies*, Washington D.C., Vol. 13.

Glenn, John (26 June, 1992), "On Proliferation Law, a Disgraceful Failure", *The Herald Tribune.*

Hagerty, Devin T. (1986), "The Development of American Defence Policy toward Pakistan, 1947-54", *Fletcher Forum,* (Summer).

Harrison, Selig S. (1983), "A Breakthrough in Afghanistan?" *Foreign Policy* (Summer).

......., (1986), "Cut a Regional Deal," *Foreign Policy* (Spring).

Hillai, A.Z. (2002), "The Costs and Benefits of the Afghan War for Pakistan". Contemporary Southeast Asia, Vol. 11 (3).

Hollen, Christopher Van (1980), "Leaning on Pakistan", *Foreign Policy* (Spring).

Isenberg, David (8 November, 1984), "The Rapid Deployment Force: The Few, The Futile, The Expendable," *Cato Institute Policy Analysis,* No. 44.

Jentleson, Bruce W. (1987), American Commitments in the Third World: Theory vs. Practice. *International Organisation*, Vol. 41.

Jillani, Anees (1991) "Pakistan and CENTO: An Historical Analysis," *Journal of South Asian and Middle Eastern Studies*, Vol. 15 (1), Fall.

Johnson, Robert (1985-86), "Exaggerating American Stakes in Third World Conflicts". *International Security*, Vol. (10).

Jr. Cushman, John H. (17 October, 1986), "U.S. Seeking Awacs for Pakistan," *New York Times.*

Jr. Nye, Joseph S (9 November, 1986), "Pakistan's Bomb Could Kill Us All," *Washington Post.*

Karp, Craig M. (1986), "The War in Afghanistan," *Foreign Affairs* (Summer).

Kempe, Frederick (9 June, 1986), "Confusion in US, Doubts in Pakistan Slowing Aid to Afghanistan Guerrillas," *Wall Street Journal.*

Khan, Dr. Rais Ahmad, (1998), "Fifty Years of Pak-US relations", *Pakistan Journal of American Studies*, Vol. 16 (1), spring.

Khan, Mohammad Ayub (1964), "The Pakistan-American Alliances: Stress and Strain". *Foreign Affairs*, Vol. 42 (2).

Kidwai, Saleem, (January-June, 1998), "US and Kashmir Issue", *Asian Studies* (Calcutta), Vol. 16 (1).

Krishna Kumar, M. K. (July-December, 1997), "The Changing Perceptions of United States towards Pakistan", *India Quarterly*, Vol. 111(3-4).

Laber, Jeri (17 October, 1986), "A Dilemma for Pakistan," *New York Times.*

Lawrence Ziring (1983), "The United States and Pakistan: Troubled Alliance," *Journal of South Asian and Middle Eastern Studies* (Summer).

Lieven, Anatol, (Jan-Feb, 2002), "The Pressures on Pakistan", *Foreign Affairs*, Vol. 18 (1).

Limaye, Satu, (1992), "Changing Place of Pakistan in US-Indian Relations", *Contemporary South Asia,* (Oxford), Vol.1 (1).

Mahapatra, Chintamani, (September, 1991), "The US Pressure on Pakistan: Kashmir's Missions to Washington", *Strategic Analysis*, Vol. 14 (6).

.........,(April, 1991), "US- Pakistan Alliance in Flux", *Strategic Analysis*, Vol.14(1).

.........,(December,1992), "US-Pak Relations: Inching Back to Normalcy?", *Strategic Analysis*, Vol. 15(9).

.........,(1993), "Withstanding the Patron's Pressure", *Strategic Analysis*, Vol. 16 (8), November pp. 861-71.

.........,(October, 1994), "American Activism in Kashmir Question", *Strategic Analysis*, Vol. 21(7).

.........,(October, 1996), "Pakistan factor in Indo-American Relations". *Strategic Analysis*, Vol. 19(7).

.........,(July, 1994), "Pak Struggle against Pressler", *Strategic Analysis*, Vol. 17(4).

Malik, Iftikhar H. (1990), "Pakistan-US Security Relationship: Testing Bilateralism". *Asian Servay*, Vol. 30 (3).

Matt, Miller (1 December, 1986), "India, Soviets Fail to Agree on Goals for Asian Strategy," *Wall Street Journal.*

McMahon, Robert J. (1986), "Eisenhower and Third World Nationalism: A Critique of the Revisionists" *Political Science Quarterly*, Vol. 101.

.........,(1988), "United States Cold War Strategy in South Asia: Making a Military Commitment to Pakistan, 1947-1954" *Journal of American History.* Vol.75.

Meltcalf, Barbara D. (September, 1984), "Government by Islam," *Worldview.*

Miller, Matt (15 April, 1986), "Bhutto Daughter Rocks Pakistan Politics," *Wall Street Journal.*

.... (19 August, 1986), "Pakistan Riots Neither Side Wanted Set Stage for Harder-Line Confrontation," *Wall Street Journal.*

Molly, Moore (12 October, 1986), "India to Buy Technology, Jet Engines from US" *Washington Post.*

Mukerjee, Delip (1986), "India and the Soviet Union," *Washington Quarterly* (Spring).

O'balance, Edgar (March, 1986), "Pakistan: On the Front Porch of Conflict," *Military Review.*

Omang, Joanne (10 October, 1985), "Secret Votes Give Afghans $300 Million," *Washington Post.*

Raman, B. (July-September, 1999), "US Attitude to Pakistan", *Indian Defence Review,* Vol. 14 (3).

Reiss, Pencer (25 August, 1986), "Bhutto's Test of Wills," *Newsweek.*

Richard M. Weintraub (31 August, 1986), "Bhutto Sows Chaos, Zia Charges," *Washington Post.*

Rizvi, Hasan Askari(May-June, 1989), "The Legacy of Military Rule in Pakistan," *Survival,* Vol.31, (3).

Robert G. Wirsing (1982), "The United States and Pakistan", *International Affairs, Royal Institute of International Affairs,* Vol. 58 (4).

........., H. Johnson (1985-1986), "Exaggerating America's Stakes in Third World Conflicts," *International Security* (Winter).

Rupert, James (January 16, 1986), Arms for Rebels Siphoned Off, *Washington Post.*

........., James (October 7, 1986), "Soviets Hold a Pakistan Card," *Washington Post.*

Sen Gupta, Prasanta, and Sanghmitra Lahiri (January-June, 1996), "Contain-ment Enterprise in the South Asian Subcontinent: From Harry S. Truman to George Bush", *Asian Studies*, Vol. 14 (1).

Singh, Anita Inder (1992), "The Limits of Super Power: The United States and South Asia" *International History Review* Vol.14.

Thomas, P, Thornton, (October, 1982). "Between the Stools: US Policy towards Pakistan in the Carter Administration," *Asian Survey*, Vol. 20(10), October.

Thornton, Thomas P (1991), "US-Pakistan Relations," *Foreign Affairs*, 68, No. 3, Summer.

.... (October, 1987), Pakistan: Internal Developments and the US Interest. Washington: Foreign Policy Institute, in Thornton, Thomas P. Between the Stools: U.S. Policy towards Pakistan in the Carter Administration, Asian Survey, Vol. 20(10), October.

.... (1989), "US-Pakistan Relations", *Foreign Affairs*, 68 (3).

Thornton, Thomas Perry (1982), "Between the Stools? US Policy towards Pakistan during the Carter Administration", *Asian Survey*, 22 (10).

Toles, Tom (1987), Mr. Gazoo: A Cartoon History of the Reagan Era, New York: Pantheon Books.

.... (1989), "The New Phase in US-Pakistani Relations", *Foreign Affairs*, 68 (3).

Unterberger, Betty Miller (1981), "American Views of Mohammed Ali Jinnah and the Pakistan Liberation Movement" *Diplomatic History, Vol 5.*

Van Hollen, Christopher, (April, 1980), "The Tilt Policy revisited: Nixon Kissinger Geopolitics and South Asia", *Asian Survey*, Vol. 20, No. 4.

Venkataramani, M.S. and Harish Chandra Arya (1996), "America's Military Alliance with Pakistan: the Evolution and Course of Uneasy Partnership", *International Studies* 8(12).

Watson, Russell and Donna Foote (7 July, 1986), "Avenging Angel," *Newsweek.*

........., (1 September, 1986), "Calling Bhutto's Bluff," *Newsweek.*

Weintraub, Richard M (5 November, 1986), "Pakistanis Deny Nuclear-Arms Report," Washington Post.

........., (8 November, 1986), "Ethnic Violence Afflicts Pakistan," *Washington Post.*

.........,.(21 September, 1986), "Pakistan's Fragile Democracy," *Washington Post.*

Weisman, Steven R. (30 October, 1986), "Civilian Areas Raided By Russians, Pakistanis Say," *New York Times.*

Weisman, Steven R. (10 August, 1986), "The Islamisation of Pakistan: Still Moving Slowly and Still Stirring Debate," *New York Times.*

........., (September, 1986), "Struggle in Pakistan: The Return of Benazir Bhutto," *New York Times.*

Wilcox, Wayne A (1965), "The Pakistan Coup d'Etat of 1958." *Pacific Affairs, Vol.* 38.

Wirsing, Robert G. (1985), "The Arms Race in South Asia: Implications for the United States", *Asian Survey*, 25 (3).

Woodward, Bob (4 November, 1986), "Pakistan Reported Near Atom Arms Production," *Washington Post.*

Newspapers/Magazines

Aslan Age (Delhl)

Boston Herald (Boston, Massachusetts)

Chicago Sun Times (Chicago)

Daily News (New York)

Daily Oklahoman (Oklahoman)

Dawn (Karachi)

Far Eastern Economic Review (Hong Kong)

Frontier Post (Peshawar)

Hindustan Times (New Delhi)
Indian Express (New Delhi).
International Herald Tribune (Paris)
Los Angeles Times (Los Angeles, California)
New York Post (New York)
New York Times (New York)
News Seattle Times (Seattle, Washington)
Newsday (New York)
Newsweek (New York)
San Antonio Express News (San Antonio, Texas)
Seattle Post Intelligencer (Washington)
The Economist (Westminster, UK)
The Express Tribune (Karachi)
The Hindu (Chennai)
The Journal News (White Plains, New York)
The Nation (Lahore)
The Nation (New York)
The News Journal (Wilmington, Ohio)
The Salt Lake Tribune (Salt Lake, Utah, USA)
The State Journal-Register (Illinois)
The Wall Street Journal (New York)
The Washington Post (Washington, D.C)
Time (New York)
Times of India (New Delhi)
USA Today (Virginia)

Websites

http://www.bbc.com
http://www.cnn.com
http://www.usaenge.org
www.afpc.org
www.cianet.org

www.foregnaffairs.org

www.foreignpolicy.com

www.fpa.com

www.hvk.org/atricles

www.ncafp.org

www.pakobsrever.net

www.pakstop.com/pakrelations

www.state.gov

www.thirdworldtravelar.com/Foreign_poliy/US_ForeignPolicy.html

www.usaid.gov/policy

www.usaid.org/policy www.usnewsclassroom.com

Index